# GOD IS RED

基
督
教

# GOD IS
# RED

*The Secret Story of How Christianity Survived
and Flourished in Communist China*

## LIAO YIWU

*Translator: Wenguang Huang*

HarperOne
*An Imprint of* HarperCollins*Publishers*

# HarperOne

All Bible references are based on The NIV Study Bible, published by Zondervan Bible Publishers in 1984.

All Chinese names in this book, including the author's, follow the Chinese tradition, with the family name written first.

HarperCollins books may be purchased for educational, business, or sales promotional use. For information please write: Special Markets Department, HarperCollins Publishers, 10 East 53rd Street, New York, NY 10022.

HarperCollins website: http://www.harpercollins.com

HarperCollins®, 📖®, and HarperOne™ are
trademarks of HarperCollins Publishers

FIRST EDITION

Library of Congress Cataloging-in-Publication Data
Liao, Yiwu.
God is red : the secret story of how Christianity survived and flourished in Communist
China / Liao Yiwu ; translated by Wenguang Huang. — 1st ed.
p. cm.
ISBN 978–0–06–207846–9
1. China—Church history—20th century. 2. Communism and Christianity—China—
History—20th century. 3. China—Church history—21st century. 4. Communism and
Christianity—China—History—21st century. I. Title.
BR1288.L68 2011
275.1'082—dc22
2010051154

11 12 13 14 15 RRD(H) 10 9 8 7 6 5 4 3 2 1

# Contents

## Part I
# THE TRIP TO DALI

## Part II
# THE YI AND MIAO VILLAGES

## Translator's Note

Liao Yiwu is one of the most prominent and outspoken contemporary writers in China today. His epic poem "Massacre," composed in 1989 in condemnation of the government's bloody crackdown at Tiananmen Square, landed him in jail for four years. His book *The Corpse Walker: Real Life Stories, China from the Bottom Up* (2008), which chronicles the lives of those on the margins of Communist society, remains banned in China. The Chinese leadership deems his writings subversive because they are critical of the socialist system.

Despite the adverse environment at home, Liao is undeterred and continues to give his curiosity full rein. In *God Is Red*, he turns his attention to an area hidden from the West for many years, one that remains a subject of immense controversy—the resurgence of Christianity in China. The World Christian Database estimates that there are seventy million practicing Christians in China. In a society tightly controlled by an atheist government, Christianity is China's largest formal religion.

The number will no doubt surprise many Westerners who are more likely to associate China with incense-burning Buddhists and Taoists, or pragmatic Confucians, or red-flag-waving Communist atheists and spiritually ambivalent converts to consumerism.

Christianity entered China as early as the seventh century, and the scientific exchanges involving Jesuits in the court of Kublai Khan are well chronicled, but the religion didn't firmly take root until the nineteenth century, when improvements in transportation and access to the interior made it possible for waves of European missionaries to work in the Middle Kingdom. Before the Communist takeover in 1949, local Chinese Christian leadership, trained abroad or tutored by missionaries, accelerated its indigenous growth. According to the China Soul for Christ Foundation, the number of followers had reached seven hundred thousand when foreign missionaries were expelled in 1949.

Before Mao Zedong's death in 1976, many Chinese Christians were imprisoned or executed. In recent years, as the government began relaxing its control over religion, Christianity underwent explosive growth, though the Communist Party sought to keep the Christian movement in check by requiring all churches to belong to either the Three-Self Patriotic Movement or the Chinese Patriotic Catholic Association. The official *China Daily* reported in 2007 that there were an estimated forty million professed Protestants and about ten million Catholics—Beijing views Catholics as separate from mainstream Christianity—in China. While a large number of Chinese chose to recognize the political reality and practiced their religion within the government's prescribed limits, others resisted, believing that only God, not the Party, could lay claim to their beliefs. They eschewed the "official" churches and gathered for worship in their homes—called the "house-church movement"—despite ongoing persecution by government authorities. The movement has been gaining momentum.

Liao's interest in Christianity began in July 1998, when he was visiting a friend in Beijing and met Xu Yonghai, a neurologist-turned-preacher with an underground Protestant church. It was the first time that Liao came into contact with a Chinese Christian. That meeting is described in a story called "The Secret Visit":

I gathered from the scraps I could catch from their conversation that they were planning to print some banned materials. Yonghai was tense and would, every few minutes, raise his head furtively and look outside to see if anyone was there. They had apparently finished their business when Yonghai moved closer to me and whispered, "We have to be careful. I think Xu Wenli's home is bugged." I nodded, acknowledging his caution.

He wanted Xu Wenli's help with a publication for China's underground church members and, warming to me, talked about the concept of salvation through God. I knew little about Christianity at the time and was interested in what he had to say, but deep down I rejected his proselytizing. In the end, I said, "I don't go to the church." He laughed, "I don't go to the church either . . . they are all government controlled."

Having grown up under the rule of Mao, when religious practices were banned and Communism was treated like a national religion with Mao at its center, deified and worshipped, Liao remained skeptical of any forms of religion. He had scant knowledge of Christianity, which had long been demonized by the government as "spiritual opium" brought in by foreign imperialists. However, for a writer who had been in and out of jail for his writings critical of the government, Liao felt strongly about freedom of expression and freedom of religion. He did not share Yonghai's faith but admired his courage.

After returning to his hometown in Sichuan, Liao began researching the Christian faith in China and learned about the underground Christian movement, of which Yonghai was at the forefront.

Liao maintained contact with Yonghai and engaged in long conversations with him about politics and faith until early 2004, when Yonghai's telephone was disconnected; Yonghai had been arrested while

preaching at a private home in China's southeastern province of Zhejiang and was sentenced to three years in prison.

Yonghai's arrest spurred Liao's interest in Christian issues. When
he traveled to Beijing again in early 2004, his friend Yu Jie, a writer
and prominent Christian activist, gave him a copy of a documentary
made by Yuan Zhiming, *The Cross: Jesus in China*. The film chronicles
the history and growth of Christianity in China and sheds some light
on early Christian martyrs and individual believers, who are part of
China's "house-church movement." Seeing the extensive footage of
large Christian gatherings was an eye-opening experience for Liao, and
he felt compelled to include Christians in his wider project about people
living at the margins of society in China today.

An opportunity presented itself in December 2004 when Liao, on
the run from government agents who had raided his apartment while
he was interviewing members of Falun Gong, a banned quasi-religious
group, went into hiding in Yunnan. In Lijiang, he met a Chinese Christian doctor, identified throughout this book by only his family name,
Sun, who gave up a lucrative city practice to do missionary work in the
remote mountainous regions of southwestern China. Since Dr. Sun's
territory covered a large swath of China's minority regions, where early
European and American Christian missionaries had been active, Liao
asked to join Dr. Sun on several monthlong journeys that took him
to villages with large populations of the Miao and Yi people, two of
China's largest ethnic groups.

In those ethnic enclaves, impoverished by isolation and largely
neglected by modernization, Liao stumbled upon a vibrant Christian
community that had sprung from the work of Western missionaries in
the late nineteenth and early twentieth centuries. Liao was granted rare
access for an outsider.

Liao interviewed Christians at a gleaming white church that
"stood proudly among the mountain peaks, with a red cross displayed

prominently on top of the steeple." He witnessed a prayer session in a crammed courtyard house where "animals and humans lived side by side, forming a harmonious picture." At services celebrated like festivals, Liao heard illiterate villagers express their love of God with eloquence.

Many of those Liao interviewed for this book had never opened up to an outsider. They shared stories about "tall and blond or red-haired" foreigners saving villages during the devastating Third Pandemic of bubonic plague that swept China and much of the world at the beginning of the twentieth century. They told how the foreigners promoted public hygiene and taught villagers how to protect their water supplies, how they spread literacy by building schools, improved health through their hospitals, and saved infants and young children abandoned by their parents because of poverty. Villagers also opened up to Liao and told him tales of brutal suppression and persecution of prominent Christian leaders in the Mao era, including the tragic and heroic story of Reverend Wang Zhiming, a Protestant minister executed during the Cultural Revolution and honored by Westminster Abbey as one of ten Christian martyrs of the past century, with a statue above the west entrance to the abbey.

Liao was moved by the sustaining power of faith and the optimistic spirit among the congregations he encountered. For example, after recounting the tragic story of Reverend Wang Zhiming, his son, Reverend Wang Zisheng, told Liao: "I don't feel bitter. As Christians, we forgive the sinner and move on to the future. We are grateful for what we have today. There is so much for us to do. In our society today, people's minds are entangled and chaotic. They need the words of the gospel now more than at any other time."

In the cities, Liao witnessed the political tensions that dog unregistered and government-sanctioned house churches but was refreshed by the more laissez-faire approach by government authorities to religion in the countryside. Villagers treated politics and religion in a more pragmatic manner. They might have been baptized at a government Three-Self Patriotic Church but would feel no qualms about praying with and listening to leaders of a house church. "The holy figure on the cross above the pulpit is my Lord, whether it was above the pulpit at a government church or inside a living room," a twenty-four-year-old man told Liao. Moreover, Liao found it common for families to display a portrait of Chairman Mao on one wall and a picture of Jesus on another.

In late spring 2009 Liao and I started discussing the possibility of developing a book based on his experiences in Yunnan. He wanted to explore the broader issue of spirituality in China in the post-Mao era, when the widespread loss of faith in Communism as well as rampant corruption and greed resulting from the country's relentless push for modernization have created a faith crisis. Though *God Is Red* takes Christianity as its subject, its objective is to delve into the past and present experiences of a particular group of people in search of clues about China's future.

In the summer of 2009 Liao went back to Yunnan and stayed for a month in the ancient section of Dali, a city well known for its diverse and robust religious culture. There he conducted a series of new interviews to expand the scope of this book. He visited the city's two oldest Christian churches built by Western missionaries at the beginning of the twentieth century and tracked down local Christian leaders and activists to record their life stories.

In *God Is Red*, Liao has brought to readers, for the first time, a collection of eighteen loosely interlinked interviews and essays written between 2002 and 2010. The past, present, and future coexist in the pages of *God Is Red*. Some stories, while unique and colorful, typify the experiences of ordinary Chinese Christians and shed light on the social and political controversies that envelop and at times overshadow the issue of Christian faith in China today. Other pieces capture the dark years of the Mao era, when the claws of political persecution left no place untouched in China and when thousands of Christians, and numberless others besides, were tortured and murdered. More important, each story puts a human face on the historical and ongoing political battles staged by ordinary people against what is still a police state.

In *God Is Red*, Liao's essays also chronicle his own transformation. He started this project as an outsider—an urban, non-Christian, Han Chinese writer—thrust into a crowd of rural ethnic Miao, Yi, and Bai Christians, whose language, cultural traditions, and faiths were foreign to him. At times, Liao felt alienated and confused. At the end of the journey, the villagers' hospitality, honesty, and sincerity, their single-minded pursuit of their faith, as well as their optimism for the future, melted away any sense of alienation and helped him gain a better understanding of China. He was deeply touched by what he heard and witnessed. In his story "The Fellowship," he observes:

> Village women, many of whom were semiliterate, had long been deprived of the right to speak and did not so much "tell" their stories as perform them, articulating their ideas with eloquence, as if each had been a professional trained actress. Their stories were told with vivid anecdotes. The variation of tone and occasional outbursts of tears enhanced the effect, carrying their performances to a high emotional level. They were true storytellers. I was a meager scribbler compared with their gift.

Even though Liao remains a "nonbeliever," the journeys brought him kinship with millions of Chinese Christians who are finding meaning in a tumultuous society, where unbridled consumerism is upending traditional and inculcated value systems. Liao saw parallels in the perseverance by Chinese Christians with his own fight for the freedom to write and travel. In September 2010, when the Chinese government finally granted Liao a permit to present his literary works and perform music in Germany after he had attempted to do so fourteen times in the previous ten years, he e-mailed his friends: "To gain and preserve your freedom and dignity, there is no other way except to fight. I will continue to write and document the sufferings of people living at the bottom rung of society, even though the Communist Party is not pleased with my writing. I have the responsibility to help the world understand the true spirit of China, which will outlast the current totalitarian government."

Wenguang Huang,
Chicago,
November 2010

# THE MOUNTAIN PATH IS RED

"Every inch of soil beneath my feet was red, shining under the frail winter sun, as if it had been soaked with blood."

I jotted down this observation in my journal in the winter of 2005 while trekking on a narrow mountain path in China's southwestern province of Yunnan.

I had arrived in Yunnan a year before, running away from public security agents who came to interrogate me for interviewing members of Falun Gong. Fear of arrest prompted me to jump from my second-floor apartment. I fled to the sun-drenched city of Dali, where I took temporary shelter at a friend's place. Like a rat sneaking out from a tight-lidded container, in this case, the Sichuan basin, I brushed off the dust, stretched my limbs on the beach of Erhai Lake, and resumed my life as a writer and musician—performing my Chinese flute on the street and in bars, and interviewing people and writing about them.

Broke and depressed in a new city, I cut myself off from my friends in Beijing and Chengdu. During the day, I roamed the streets, hanging out with beggars, street vendors, musicians, and prostitutes, listening to their life stories. In the evenings, I doused my loneliness with liquor, through which I even made an unexpected acquaintance with plainclothes police officers who had been sent to monitor my activities. Unlike those in Sichuan, policemen in Yunnan never refused a free drink and felt no qualms about being my drinking buddies. Even in their highly intoxicated state, they didn't forget to toe the Party line by saying how hard they tried to protect the Communist system, and that it was good for China. But drinking was not an effective escape and even worsened my sense of loneliness.

Then, at the end of 2004, l met a Christian, known among local villagers as Dr. Sun, a medical doctor. Following his conversion to Christianity, he quit his position as the dean of a large medical school near Shanghai and came to the rural areas of Yunnan, healing the sick and spreading the gospel. On that day, he was performing a cataract surgery inside my friend's shanty house in Lijiang. The patient was an old lady who was too poor to pay for the procedure at the government-run hospital.

The bespectacled Dr. Sun, in a casual green jacket and a white T-shirt, looked more like a schoolteacher than a surgeon. With thin hair on top, he reminded me of Xu Yonghai, a neurologist-turned-preacher whom I had met six years before in Beijing. Yonghai, an activist with the government-banned "house-church movement," had been imprisoned a few months previously for preaching in the southeastern province of Zhejiang. On this particular day, Dr. Sun did not proselytize.

To my surprise, he said he had read my books—pirated versions that he had managed to purchase on the street. As he politely complimented me on my literary efforts, I was beginning to wonder what it was in Christianity that had driven these successful medical doctors to abandon their lucrative careers in the big cities to pursue a life filled with risks and hardships. When I asked Dr. Sun for permission to interview him, he initially declined. "I've led an ordinary life," he said humbly. "If you are interested, come with me to the mountains. You will discover extraordinary stories in the villages there."

Of course I was interested. I had spent the better half of my life capturing extraordinary stories from ordinary people.

One year later, in December 2005, Dr. Sun and I met in Kunming, the capital of Yunnan and set out on a monthlong journey that took us deep into the mountains, first by bus and then on a small tractor, along perilous mountain paths paved with small rocks, which the locals call "hard candies." We passed Fumin and Luquan counties, both of which I had never heard of, and then Sayingpan Township, where the paved roads ended. Trudging along on winding red-mud trails, we reached a cluster of small villages hemmed in by tall mountains. According to Dr. Sun, there was a vibrant Christian community there.

The place reminded me of an old Chinese saying: "Heaven is high above and the emperor is far away," which refers to regions that are so distant and isolated that they seem to fall beyond the reach of both divine and secular powers. I wondered how it was possible for Christianity, a foreign faith, to find its way and grow in such isolated locations, where the vast modernization that was sweeping other parts of China had not yet reached. Peasants still eked out a meager living by plowing tiny plots of terraced land with hoes and shovels. Television was still a luxury, and many had never heard of refrigerators, not to mention computers or the Internet. Medical care was almost nonexistent—for example, when one of the villagers fell sick, it took his relatives six hours to carry him to the nearest hospital. En route, on the bumpy road, he expired. The itinerant medical service of Dr. Sun was the only hope for the inhabitants of those remote villages.

In the subsequent days after I started talking with some of the villagers, my initial assumptions gradually changed. It was true that people in the cold, high plateau of Yunnan were cut off from the developed urban centers and were destitute. However, on a deeper level, the region was never immune from both the political and cultural influences of the outside world. In fact, this region was well within the grasp of both divine and secular powers.

In the village of Zehei, inhabited by China's ethnic Yi people, locals led me to the muddy hut of Zhang Yingrong, an eighty-six-year-old church elder whose peaceful and benevolent looks made me think of my late father. Zhang Yingrong talked fondly about the London-based China Inland Mission that had sent its first group of missionaries to Shanghai more than 150 years ago. At that time, several of these nineteenth-century missionaries set their sights on the Yi villages hidden up in the mountains. Because modern transportation was lacking, these foreigners, with "blond hair and big noses," rode on donkeys, journeying for many days to reach the region, just in time to save the mountain people from a devastating bubonic epidemic, using Western medicine and their knowledge of modern hygienic practices. They also brought with them, in their inexact Mandarin translations, copies of the Shengjing—the Bible. The Word of God, Zhang Yingrong said, gradually penetrated the whole region by winning the hearts and minds of villagers who for generations had found solace in the chanting of local shamans and the worshipping of pagan gods. Zhang Yingrong's father was among the early followers and then brought his whole family along. The missionaries eventually established schools and hospitals. At an early age, Zhang Yingrong attended the Southwestern Theology Seminary, and before he reached twenty, he was ready to follow in the missionaries' footsteps.

Zhang Yingrong's captivating stories piqued my interest in Christianity about which I knew very little. I grew up in the era when Western missionaries were portrayed as "evil agents of the imperialists," who enslaved the Chinese mind, killed Chinese babies, and ruined indigenous cultures. I decided to talk with some local Christians, and under Dr. Sun's guidance, I ventured deeper into the mountain valleys.

Another Christian leader, Reverend Wang Zisheng, an ethnic Miao, lived in a village across a river. He recounted a similar tale about the blue-eyed missionaries who saved lives and spread the words of the gospel. So did Reverend Zhang Mao-en in Salaowu. As the interviews progressed, I found a pattern—locals had inherited their Christian faith from their parents and grandparents who had benefited from the teachings of a certain foreign missionary. Was the missionary English, French, German, American, Australian, or New Zealander? They didn't know. To them, it was not important. Through the efforts of that foreign missionary, who had found a fertile ground in which to plant the seeds of faith, Christianity had taken root earlier than it had in other parts of China. Three or four generations later, Christianity was part of the heritage of each individual family and an integral part of local history.

It was a path filled with strife and blood.

"Sometimes, devils often follow the footsteps of God to undo his work," a local Christian whispered to me, referring to the period in the 1940s when the Communists forced their way in there and Mao Zedong's atheist ideology clashed violently with the Christian faith. Zhang Yingrong, who was a preacher in training when the Communists initiated the land redistribution campaign in 1950, was labeled a "landlord" even though he had no properties in his name. The ruthless beatings, the forced kneeling on broken tiles in the pouring rain, and the near starvation reduced him to a state of near paralysis for a number of years.

Another preacher, Wang Zhiming, led the Christian movement after the Western missionaries had retreated from China. In the 1950s, local Communist officials closed the church and sent him to work in the field to be reeducated. He quietly accepted the reality of being under Communism and temporarily ceased his church activities. During the Cultural Revolution, when the Party infringed on his bottom line—that is, denied him the right to pray—he acted in defiance and was willing to give up his life. As expected, he was arrested while leading a prayer session inside a mountain cave and was brutally executed following a public condemnation meeting, with his tongue cut out of his mouth to prevent him from preaching.

In the Mao era, local Christians were not allowed to pray and attend church and were forced to accept the Communist ideology. They complied, but only a few openly denounced their faith. In order to protect their faith from being totally suppressed in that region, some brave Christians gathered for services inside mountain caves. As a result, Christianity survived, and a few years after Mao Zedong's death, it came back again with a vengeance. Village after village became Christian territory.

On that journey to the Yi people, I attended a Eucharist celebration, which locals celebrated like a holiday, slaughtering pigs and chickens for a sumptuous feast.

I grew up in the cities, where Christianity has also revived and flourished in the post-Mao era but with a distinctive foreign identity. Many new converts are highly educated and well-off professionals or retirees. They have embraced Christianity the way they do Coca-Cola or a Volkswagen—believing that a foreign faith, like foreign-made products, has better quality. Many younger urban Christians have been throwing themselves at the feet of Jesus because it is considered hip to wear a cross and sing a foreign-sounding hymn.

In the Yi and Miao villages, Christianity is now as indigenous as qiaoba, a special Yi buckwheat cake. A majority of the Christians I met were poor illiterate farmers who had nothing to share with a visitor, but a wealth of stories. Like qiaoba, Christianity is life-sustaining to the Yi. For Reverend Wang Zisheng and church elder Zhang Yingrong, faith enabled them to survive the brutal persecution during the dark years under Mao. For Zhang Meizhi, who lost her husband, brothers, and sons to Mao's political campaigns, a recent conversion to Christianity lifted her anger and finally gave her some peace. For a villager who had been ostracized after killing a snake, which the locals believed could cause leprosy, his newly acquired Christian faith put him in the midst of a large and welcoming community.

In the urban metropolises of China, will Christianity provide a spiritual haven that calms the restless populace caught up in the relentless pursuit of wealth and material comfort? It has certainly changed the lives of Dr. Xu Yonghai and Dr. Sun. Or will the Christian faith, like Buddhism and Taoism, make people more submissive to totalitarian power? There is an ongoing debate among Chinese scholars as to whether some Christians forgave the murderous government as a genuine display of God's benevolence—or as an excuse for cowardice. As the Party continues to persecute Christians, and keeps a wary eye on any spiritual movement that might challenge its authority, the willingness of Christians to forgive, however, is not universal. When I asked a centenarian nun if she was willing to pray and forgive the Communist government, which had destroyed her church, she jumped up from her seat and stamped her feet emphatically, "No, certainly not! They still occupy our church property! I refuse to die! I will wait until they return everything back to the church!"

After I came back from the trip with Dr. Sun, I became preoccupied with the topic. To continue my research of Christianity in Yunnan, I went back to Dali again in 2009 to trace the footsteps of early Christian missionaries, many of whom had settled there and used the city as a launching pad for their missions in places farther away. These trips have exhilarated me, lifting me out of my drunken depression. The stories of heroic Christians like Zhang Yingrong, Reverend Wang Zhiming, and Dr. Sun have inspired me, prompting me to write a book during a time when East and West are meeting and clashing on many fronts. In these remote corners, I have discovered a center point, where East met West, and although there has been a collision of cultures, there is now a new Christian identity that is distinctively Chinese.

The circuitous mountain path in Yunnan province is red because over many years it has been soaked with blood.

Liao Yiwu,
Chengdu, Sichuan province,
November 2010

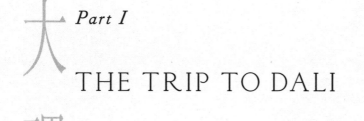

*Part I*

# THE TRIP TO DALI

*Chapter 1*

## THE CEMETERY

Ze Yu looked like one of those smiley, big-bellied Buddhist statues found in restaurants all over China—benevolent, round face, shaved head, rotund, and triple chinned. He's a monk and knows all the jokes. And when I suggested he could be the Maitreya, the Buddha yet to come, he responded with a good-humored laugh and said that we, that is, my mother and I, were just in time for lunch and led us into the old part of Dali City in the southwestern province of Yunnan. My watch showed just past noon. It was August 3, 2009, and we had traveled two days and a night from Chengdu in neighboring Sichuan province to stay at a courtyard house lent to us by my friend, the avant-garde poet Ye Fu, in a rural village at the foot of Cangshan Mountain.

We ate in a Muslim halal restaurant. A painting of pilgrims in Mecca hung in the main serving hall. We ordered beef and lamb while Monk Ze extolled its range of vegetarian dishes. As we chatted, we talked about "Charter 08," the manifesto to promote political reforms and human rights in China, of which he is a signatory. I saluted his courage but wondered whether a monk shouldn't stay out of politics. His happy face became earnest: "Without democracy, Buddhism won't survive here."

As we walked off lunch in the old city, Ze pointed out little details, missed by the average tourist, that brought to life Dali's thousand years of history. The old city was small by Chinese standards—only three or four kilometers from one end to the other, with a permanent population of thirty to forty thousand. But concentrated here were worshippers of many gods and deities. The indigenous Bai people venerated thousands of them in their temples, from the legendary Dragon King of the Eastern China Sea and the Queen Mother of Heaven to ancient emperors and warriors. He showed us Muslim mosques and Buddhist temples and Christian churches, both Catholic and Protestant. Less conspicuous, he said, were the practitioners of Bahá'í and Falun Gong, who used their homes, as did those Christians who refused to recognize government-sanctioned churches.

Since it was the Christians who had stirred my curiosity, Ze wanted to show me a well-known cemetery for Western missionaries who had journeyed into China more than a century before. He believed I might learn something. And so, a few days later, after much walking along mountain paths and several bus rides, Ze and I reached Wuliqiao Village. After more walking, mostly uphill, we stood under a blazing sun at the edge of a cemetery. "Here?" I asked, but Ze shook his head. This, he said, was for Muslims, primarily ethnic Hui. I knew about the Muslim rebellion against Chinese rule in the mid-nineteenth century and the violence that swept Dali. Many Han and Bai were slaughtered. The Qing emperor sent troops and brutally suppressed the Muslim uprising with thousands of casualties. The cemetery was bounded by a stone wall. "Only Muslim ghosts are allowed in here," Ze said. With suppression of the Muslim rebellion came a period of calm, and it was during the lull that missionaries from, among others, the China Inland Mission, poured into the area.

"We are close," Ze said and kept walking. After about three hundred more meters the road dead-ended in thick waist-deep cannabis plants and fragrant herbs. We found a side path that led to a tall ridge, and from that vantage point Ze swept his arm to take in five plots of corn in the middle of which stood an excavator, its metallic arm convulsing like the leg of a giant cockroach. "There," he said, "is the missionary cemetery."

We zigzagged our way down on a steep path, arms outstretched like birds to keep our balance, but I could yet see no sign of a cemetery. The excavator lifted its arm and struck the earth, lift and strike, lift, strike. "Are they renovating the cemetery?" I asked. Ze gave me a cynical laugh. "You may wish. They are extracting the headstones. High quality rock, much sought after by property developers." As I looked down at the uneven ground beneath my feet, I could see broken and jagged pieces of stone and, as I focused on the pieces, groups of letters from the Roman alphabet and then whole words, in English, and crosses.

We found the foundations of the cemetery wall and managed to pace out two equal squares, each of about half an acre. Space enough for the bodies of many foreign or Chinese Christians, but no complete records have survived to say just how many.

My research told me this: British missionary George Clarke purchased the land and built the cemetery. Clarke's Chinese name was Hua Guoxiang, which means fragrance of blossom and fruits. An active member of the London-based China Inland Mission since 1865, Clarke left England in 1881 with his Swiss wife, Fanny, and reached the ancient city of Dali via Myanmar and Guizhou province.

George and Fanny Clarke were almost certainly the earliest missionaries in the region. Initially, they printed Christian pamphlets and gave them out at markets and along the roadside. They also distributed candies to children. But they soon realized that their pamphlets were largely useless because most Bai villagers were illiterate, and their own Mandarin Chinese was of little use in communicating with people who spoke only Bai. So they set about learning Bai while initiating literacy programs in the villages and teaching people to sing hymns in Chinese. They also learned how to imitate the Bai ancestor-worshipping dances and incorporated some of that culture into their Christian teachings. Soon, the Clarkes dressed up in Bai costumes and danced to the rhythms of gongs and drums on the street to attract people and spread the gospel. They wrote up hymns using a popular form of local ditty. I heard stories about how the Clarkes would visit the Bai villages to spend time with musicians and were seen dancing on moonlit nights near Erhai Lake.

The Clarkes lived in Dali for two years but had limited success. They set up a boarding school but attracted only three students. Fanny became pregnant and gave birth to a son. They named him Samuel Dali Clarke.

Two months after giving birth, Fanny became seriously ill. News of her illness spread quickly among her Chinese neighbors, who came to console her. They were deeply touched by her beautiful voice and by the optimism she showed during her illness. She had left instructions with her husband that she be buried in Dali so she could be part of Cangshan Mountain and Erhai Lake. Her devotion inspired people around her and after her death, many of their Chinese friends and neighbors flocked to the church and were baptized.

So began the Christian cemetery at the foot of Cangshan Mountain. On the walls that fenced the cemetery, craftsmen engraved crosses and biblical verses in both Chinese and English. George Clarke buried his wife on the morning of October 30, 1883. It was the first such funeral the indigenous people had ever seen—to them, sending off the dead involved incense burning, sutra chanting, and shaman dancing. They were now being asked to understand that Fanny's soul was ascending to heaven, where she would be with God.

In the ensuing years, at least fifty foreign Christians served the communities in Dali. According to *The History of Christianity in Dali,* written and self-published in 2005 by Wu Yongsheng, between 1881 and 1949 the city became an important Christian base in southwest China.

In the beautiful land dotted with lakes and hemmed in by mountains, churches sprung up across the countryside, attracting more than a hundred thousand followers. Missionaries built hospitals, orphanages, and schools.

I was struck by the dedication of the missionaries. One such story relates to a Canadian missionary doctor, Jessie McDonald. She came to China in 1913 and worked at a hospital in China's central city of Kaifeng, Henan province. In 1940, when Kaifeng fell to Japanese forces, she moved the hospital southwest to Dali, where she established the Gospel Hospital. Her work came to an abrupt end on May 4, 1951, when Communist officials seized the hospital and its equipment and ordered McDonald out of China. A big Red Cross symbol on the front wall of the hospital was painted over with a slogan: "Kicking imperialists out of China." Many Christian followers became scared; they either quit the church or publicly renounced their faith. McDonald is said to have been the last foreign missionary to leave China, and on her last day she ignored the threats of soldiers and went to pray at what is now the Old City Protestant Church, built by missionaries in 1905. She was alone in the church, surrounded by empty pews.

At the top of the church's dome was a clock weighing 150 kilograms and modeled on London's Big Ben. Its bell was commissioned by Richard Williams and William J. Embery, who personally delivered the bell via sea to Saigon, Vietnam, from where it was taken along the Mekong River to Yunnan and on to Dali. The entire journey took three months.

McDonald made for the bell and struck it for the last time. The sound rippled through the city. Three old men drinking tea in the old city remember it. "The chiming came in waves, resounding waves, one after another; people in Xiaguan could feel the vibration," said one.

On the afternoon of January 28, 1998, a couple from France, descendants of George and Fanny Clarke, were met in Dali by Wu Yongsheng. The couple had been inspired after reading Alvyn Austin's history of the China Inland Mission, *China's Millions*, and wanted to visit where their great-grandparents were buried.

That story reminds me of lines from a poem by Paul Valery, "The Graveyard by the Sea":

> *But in their heavy night, cumbered with marble,*
> *Under the roots of trees a shadow people*
> *Has slowly now come over to your side.*

The poet returns in his imagination to the cemetery of Sète, his hometown on the Mediterranean. He is sitting on a tombstone at noon, staring out on a calm sea, contemplating life and death. But things are rarely as we imagine them to be, and though the French couple may have been expecting a slice of China's natural beauty, the scene they came across in 1998 was much the same as the one I encountered a decade later. No cemetery, no garden, just an empty, albeit rocky, field plowed for planting. Wu told me the villagers gathered around the French visitors and attempted to recount what had happened to the graves. One said that during the Cultural Revolution the Red Guards often used the cemetery as a target in their fight against foreign imperialists, waving red flags, shouting slogans, and singing revolutionary songs. They ransacked the cemetery, again and again, claiming that they would wipe out the ancestral graves of imperialists. Another villager recalled that the Red Guards had used explosives on the gravestones and blown them into pieces. Another said destruction of the cemetery started way back in the 1950s; with each political campaign, the cemetery became a target of hatred toward foreign imperialists. That didn't take into account local pillaging; headstones and markers were recycled as pigsties, courtyard walls, and the footings for numerous houses. Even before the Cultural Revolution started, half of the graves had been leveled. The missionaries' cemetery was one more desecration in the name of Communism that trashed China's treasure troves of history.

The French couple didn't find the grave of Fanny Clarke. But they had to have been heartened that she survived in the stories the local villagers told from one generation to the next. I'm moved to quote Paul Valery again:

> *The wind is rising! . . . We must try to live!*
> *The huge air opens and shuts my book: the wave*
> *Dares to explode out of the rocks in reeking*
> *Spray. Fly away, my sun-bewildered pages!*

Wu says the couple picked wildflowers and wove them into a wreath, which they placed in the middle of the cornfield. They had with them a small accordion, and the woman began to sing a song she said was Fanny Clarke's favorite. When Wu told me about the song, I recognized it right away. It was from an 1805 poem by Thomas Moore that has remained popular with singers and composers and even Hollywood:

> *'Tis the last rose of summer*
> *Left blooming alone;*
> *All her lovely companions*
> *Are faded and gone;*
> *No flower of her kindred,*
> *No rosebud is nigh.*
> *To reflect back her blushes,*
> *To give sigh for sigh.*

Here I was at the same place eleven years later. It was approaching dusk. The song was in my head, and I swayed to the rhythm of an unseen accordion. "It's time to go," Ze said. We retraced our steps, back aboard buses, back through cannabis bushes, back to the highway. I could see the steeple of a church, and a new crescent moon had risen with the stars. I could hear hymn singing off in the distance.

*Chapter 2*

## THE OLD NUN

Zhang Yinxian was fast for someone who was more than a hundred years old, and as I caught up with her in the churchyard in the old section of Dali, it occurred to me that she looked every bit like a piece of fresh ginseng, slightly crooked but full of life and energy. She ignored me as I followed her around, trying to ingratiate myself, and finally declared in words I found hard to understand that she was too busy to talk. "She's quite a celebrity around here," said the friend who had invited me and two other writers in August 2008 to Weibo Mountain to visit the old Roman Catholic church on Renmin Avenue, where an old school chum of his was a priest.

Sister Zhang stuck in my mind, and a week later I tracked her down again at the church, but it was soon apparent that her heavy Yunnan accent and partial deafness was going to make any meaningful conversation impossible. My shouting and gesturing drew the attention of some other nuns, the youngest I guessed to be in her seventies, and she began to interrogate me: Where are you from? What do you want? Are you a parishioner? Are you a Christian? I told her I was a writer and wanted to interview Sister Zhang. "Do you mean you are a journalist or something?" she asked and told me I would have to leave and get a letter of approval from the local Religious Affairs Office. Chastened, I left.

I visited Dali again the following year and, having learned my lesson, took a more cautious approach, spending a couple of days gathering more information about the church and Sister Zhang. I also enlisted the help of my friend Kun Peng, who was a Christian and well versed in theology. Kun had a contact, Sister Tao, who was in her midthirties and had bright eyes that beamed kindness. She took care of Sister Zhang and said she would try to arrange my interview and act as interpreter.

Kun and I returned the following Sunday after morning Mass and were directed to a conference room, where, after about an hour, Sister Tao appeared with Sister Zhang, serving as a fluent and necessary interpreter; I found it hard to understand Sister Zhang. "Sister Zhang has lost all her teeth," Sister Tao said. "She is quick tempered and has a loud voice. For people from out of town, it does sound like she is yelling in a foreign language."

Throughout the interview, Sister Tao sat close to her charge, a little behind and to her right. Sister Zhang was deaf in her left ear and the vision in her left eye was impaired, but it soon became clear she possessed an amazing memory, and on topics about which she had particularly strong opinions, she would stand and stomp her feet, reminding me a little of Shakespeare's King Lear railing against the elements. Sister Zhang was mad, yes, but not from any madness.

Our conversation was fast paced, but when I suggested we take a break to let Sister Zhang rest, Sister Tao said it was unnecessary. "She's much tougher than you think. Sister Zhang cooks her own meals and has a very healthy appetite." At one point, when we were talking about her state of health, Sister Zhang went over to a large heavy flowerpot and moved it across the room. We all laughed and I noticed that Sister Zhang's laugh was like that of a child, flowing freely, and the wrinkles on her face almost vanished.

Sister Zhang showed me three crosses that she carried with her, one she'd had for some sixty years. We spoke for two hours, at which point

Sister Tao suggested we wind things up because it was time for lunch. Sister Zhang did not want to leave. When we tried to lift her out of the chair, she brushed us off and continued talking, repeatedly sweeping her hands through the air. I couldn't understand what she was trying to say and turned to Sister Tao for help. "She is still pouting about the fact that a large plot of the land that had belonged to the church was seized by the government during the Cultural Revolution," Sister Tao said. "She wants it back. She wants to witness the return of the land before she leaves this world." One of those old sayings came to mind: "People with a quick temper have a short life." I thought Sister Zhang was clearly an exception.

*Liao Yiwu:* I've been looking forward to talking with you for quite some time.

*Zhang Yinxian:* I'm here in the church every day, praying, cooking, exercising, gardening, loosening up the dirt for ants and worms. If I'm not around, it means I'm out buying vegetables at the market.

*Liao:* When were you born?

*Zhang:* I was born on August 3, 1908 in Qujingcheng, Yunnan province. I don't even remember what my parents looked like. They died when I was only three. I was an orphan. I had a brother. He was taken away by a local warlord. I think he died on a battlefield. I was sent by an uncle to Kunming to serve the Lord.

*Liao:* Your uncle?

*Zhang:* He was a priest. In the Qing dynasty, under Emperor Tongzhi [1856–75], Catholic missionaries came to Yunnan from Vietnam. When I was growing up, there were many foreign missionaries, from France in particular. I was taught to read and write. I learned the Bible, attended Mass, and said prayers.

Sometimes, I would do odd jobs. Around that time, people suffered terribly. The small monastery sheltered me from the chaos outside.

When I turned thirteen, I followed my aunt to Dali. Back then, the city's old section had several churches. Then more Catholic missionaries arrived. They represented many different religious orders—Jesuits, Paulists, Franciscans, and so on. Our diocese expanded fast, into the Lijiang, Baoshan, Diqing, Lincang, Dehong, and Xishuangbanna regions. At its peak, we had more than eighty thousand parishioners from all ethnic groups—Han, Bai, Tibetan, Yi, Dai, Jingpo. Did I leave anybody out? Anyway, to accommodate the growth, the Missionaries of the Sacred Heart bought a large swath of land in the 1920s. They put a French bishop in charge. His Chinese name was Ye Meizhang. Under his leadership, the organization built a monastery, an orphanage, and this church here.

At that time, we had about four hundred people living inside the church, and on Sundays, local residents flooded in for Mass from all over. The church couldn't hold that many people. Some ended up standing or kneeling outside in the yard. Children came with their parents. When they became bored, they would climb up the trees.

Since I joined the church at an early age, I knew all the hymns, and when the priest quoted a Bible passage, I could immediately tell you chapter and verse, and I knew all the stories associated with that reference. People always complimented me, saying how smart I was, but my aunt would give me a stern look and say, "Hey, don't be such a show-off."

*Liao:* I grew up in the 1960s. My generation was told that religion was the tool employed by the imperialists to enslave people and that the nuns conducted medical experiments on children in foreign orphanages.

*Zhang:* Lies, lies. At public denunciation meetings during the Cultural Revolution, we were accused of murdering orphans. They said the priests were vampires.

In times of famine or war, poor people would abandon their children on the roadside. Some would pick a nice moonlit night, cover the baby with layers of clothes, and leave it at the church entrance. When the nuns found the baby, they would take the child in, no matter whether the baby was healthy or ill. Some parents were quite shrewd. They would leave their child with us and come back after the hard time was over. But the majority of the children here were never reclaimed. Back then, people were poor, and it was common for one family to have many children. Parents treated their babies like little animals. If they were strong and survived, they would keep them. If the babies were sick, parents would abandon them to strangers or just leave them to die.

I have seen many such cases, especially baby girls. They were abandoned by the side of the mountain path or on the beach. Lucky ones were picked up by passersby, but many became the victims of wild animals, like dogs. For baby boys, if they were born with deformities or illness, they were subject to the same fate as girls. When nuns saw an abandoned baby outside, they would bring her to the priest or bishop who knew Western medicine. If the baby had been left out for a short time, there was hope. Those who had been left outside for a long time, their arms or legs would have been ripped apart by wild animals. The chances for survival were quite small. When a baby died, we would say prayers and then bury him or her in the Catholic

cemetery. It's on the south side of Wuliqiao Village, the one that
has been destroyed.

*Liao:* I visited the cemetery. It's a cornfield now.

*Zhang:* Actually, there used to be two cemeteries there, one for the
Catholics and the other for Protestants. The two were located
next to each other. Both have been destroyed now. We can't even
get the land back from the government. Many local Catholics
were buried down there. So were the abandoned children we
weren't able to save. Those poor babies! We would hold a simple
ceremony and give them a proper burial. In the cemeteries, we
set up grave markers for everyone, whether you were a bishop, a
priest, a nun, a monk, a parishioner, or an abandoned baby. On
their tombstones, you would find inscriptions of their names,
dates of birth and death, that sort of thing.

*Liao:* How would you find out the names of those abandoned
babies?

*Zhang:* If it wasn't with the baby, the nun who found it would come
up with a name, be it Chinese or French. Then we would list
when and where we found her.

By the 1940s, our church had adopted more than two hundred
orphans. The majority of nuns became full-time nannies. Those
who had medical training turned themselves into pediatricians.
My job was to work in the kitchen, heating up milk, cooking
rice congee. Sometimes, we would have four or five abandoned
babies brought in on one day. They were so hungry. I think a
couple of the former orphans still live around here. They'd be in
their seventies or eighties now. But despite the changing political
environment, they still won't admit their relations with the
church.

*Liao:* Why is that?

*Zhang:* They renounced the church during the Cultural Revolution, afraid they would be accused of colluding with foreign imperialists. Even now, despite the situation having made a turn for the better over the past decade, they are probably still afraid of being persecuted.

Looking back on the first half of my life, I was truly happy. Every day, the church would be hustle-bustling with people. In the fall, when the breezes blew the leaves off the trees—dear God—the ground was covered with a layer of gold. During prayers or Mass, the church was packed with parishioners, but at other times this whole yard was quiet, a place of happy tranquility. In the old days, our church was big, and I was so busy every day that my back hurt all the time. My favorite job was to clean the inside of the church, dusting the altar, the pews, and the statues. We had over a dozen priests from France, Switzerland, and Belgium. If I did something wrong, they would tease me by saying: "As punishment, you need to sing three hymns—solo." They would join me, and we would have a hymn-singing contest.

*Liao:* What about the second half of your life?

*Zhang:* In August 1949, on the eve of the Communist takeover, a Swedish priest, Father Maurice Toruay—I can't believe I still remember his name—traveled to the Cizhong region [near Tibet] to preach the gospel. He was shot and killed. The news hit us hard. It was like hearing the sinister caws of dark ravens. We could sense the danger lurking ahead of us. We all knelt and prayed for protection in the new era. During a special Mass, we braced ourselves for the suffering we knew would come. We were ready to follow the steps of Father Toruay and sacrifice our lives if necessary to glorify the work of the Lord. We knew the road ahead wasn't going to be easy, but we were prepared.

Soon, the Communist troops moved into the city. People waved red flags and beat drums and gongs to welcome the soldiers. The whole country turned "red." The mountains and the Erhai Lake turned "red." Even the church was decorated with red flags and Chairman Mao's portraits. Foreign missionaries were segregated in a row of small rooms with curtains drawn. The soldiers guarded their doors, and nobody was allowed to get close to them.

*Liao:* What year was that?

*Zhang:* It was in 1952. By February that year, all the foreigners had gone.

*Liao:* Did you hold a last Mass or something to see them off?

*Zhang:* No. The chapel was sealed and no one was allowed to enter. After the foreigners left, everyone at the church had to go through a political review process. Both laity and clergy were scared and quit in droves. They answered the government's call and went home to farm. Some openly renounced the church. They said, "I will listen to the words of Chairman Mao and cut off all my ties with the Catholic Church which enslaves people." The government targeted church assets all over China. Foreign bishops were forced to hand everything over to the new government, to sign documents prepared in advance. They said church property had been obtained through the exploitation of the masses. Just like that, all the assets were seized.

I can never forget 1952, the year when the church was left empty. It used to be so glorious. Overnight, everything was gone. Rats took over the place. We used to have four hundred people working at the church. Only three were left—me, my aunt, and Bishop Liu Hanchen. We were ordered out. Bishop Liu argued and refused to leave. "The church is our home and we don't have anywhere to go."

Initially, they allowed us to stay. At the end of the year members of the local militia came with guns and took us to a village at the foot of Cangshan Mountain. Local officials held a public meeting, announcing that we would be put under the supervision of villagers there. They ordered us to engage in physical labor and reform our thinking. They built an elementary school and a high school on the land they had taken from the church and converted the monastery into housing for government officials.

*Liao:* So, you became a farmer.

*Zhang:* A low-class citizen trampled on by the masses.

*Liao:* For how many years?

*Zhang:* From 1952 to 1983. That's thirty-one years, isn't it?

*Liao:* How did you manage to survive?

*Zhang:* We grew our own crops and vegetables to support ourselves. When we left the church, we weren't allowed to bring anything with us. We walked all the way to the village, and before we even had a drink of water, the local leaders dragged us to a public denunciation meeting. They paraded us around in the village, along with some Buddhist monks and nuns, Taoist priests, and several leaders of the local Protestant churches. We were ordered to stand in three rows in front of a stage. We faced hundreds of villagers with raised fists shouting revolutionary slogans. Some spat at us. Such hatred. As the leader worked up the crowd, a peasant activist came up and slapped Bishop Liu on the face. My aunt stepped forward. "How dare you slap him." The activist used to be a poor farmer, and when the Communists confiscated the property of landowners, he was one of the beneficiaries. He pointed at my aunt and yelled back, "You are a counterrevolutionary and we have defeated you. You are the lackey of the imperialists who exploited us." My aunt said, "We are not. We came from poor families and we've never exploited anybody." The activist shouted again, "You are still stubborn and won't admit your defeat. You need to be punished." Fists were raised and the crowd began chanting, "Down with the counterrevolutionary nun!" My aunt wouldn't back down. She said to her abuser, "Slap me if you want. If you slap me on the left side of my face, I will give you the right side too."

*Liao:* Turning the other cheek . . .

*Zhang:* Those guys had no idea what my aunt meant. We had to endure many more political meetings, but after a while the humiliating remarks or beatings didn't bother us anymore. We became smarter. We learned how to protect ourselves. All of those campaigns, whether to denounce the landowners, Buddhists, Catholics, or intellectuals, were all the same. People would shout slogans—"Down with so and so!" "Beat Liu so he can never stand up!" "Long live Chairman Mao!" "Long live the Communist Party!" "Long live the victory of whatever!"—and each time, we were made to confess. It got so we knew it by rote; all we did was change a few words.

*Liao:* What was it like living in the village?

*Zhang:* The village put us in a stone house with two rooms, which were very drafty. It was more like a pigsty than a house. The new life was really hard for Bishop Liu and my aunt; they were both quite old. I was relatively young. So I went to the village leader and asked for pots and pans, some grain, and bedding. He made me sign a piece of paper, saying I would pay them back after I earned enough money.

What followed was hard labor. The farmwork wasn't that difficult, but you had to have enough physical strength. I did most of the farming. My aunt and Bishop Liu assisted me. When there were no public denunciation meetings, we were allowed to

live our life quietly. The village lent us an ox so we could plow
the field. We also raised pigs and chickens and grew vegetables.
We pickled surplus vegetables and would sell them, and eggs, at
the local market. With the money we got, we bought vegetable
oil, soy sauce, that sort of thing. Life was hard, but we got by, and
soon we could breathe a little more easily.

*Liao:* Then, of course, came the Great Leap Forward . . .

*Zhang:* We all went up on the mountains to cut down trees to fuel
the backyard furnaces making iron and steel. We were all told
that if we worked hard, China could become an industrialized
nation in two to three years. In the village, we had to hand over
everything, including our cooking utensils. But nobody took care
of the crops. Famine arrived. So many people died—it was really,
really horrible. We lived on thin corn broth, almost as clear as
plain water. Under the sun, you could see its reflection at the
bottom of the bowl; it looked like an egg yolk. Bishop Liu used
to joke that a drawing of an egg was better than no egg at all, and
my aunt would cup the bowl in her hand and say, seriously, "We
are eating the sunny egg broth offered by the Lord. I'm sure the
broth in this bowl has more nutrients."

Pretty soon, there was nothing left. We had to search for food
in the mountains. We looked for wild vegetables, grass roots,
moss, even tree bark. Some of the villagers were so desperate,
they dug up dead bodies and feasted on the flesh. Even Buddhist
monks hunted and ate rats. Let me tell you, there was chaos
everywhere. Had the famine lasted much longer, I'm sure the
villagers would have eaten us. Thank the Lord we survived.

We prayed—on the road, climbing a hill, at home. We had
all spent many years reading the Bible, and God's words were
etched, stroke by stroke, on my mind and in my heart. No matter
how hard the government tried, those words couldn't be erased.

When we felt dizzy from hunger, we never asked for help, because they couldn't even save themselves. We prayed that the Lord would grant us peace.

One day, I joined other villagers combing an area in the mountains for food. Almost half a day had gone and I hadn't found anything. I was exhausted and fell to ground and could not get up again. That's when I noticed some colorful wild mushrooms near me. Those were the poisonous ones that nobody dared to touch. Hunger weakened my will and judgment. I snatched the mushrooms and put them into my mouth. I grew up in the region and knew the terrible consequences of swallowing poisonous mushrooms. Oh well, if I had to choose between death from hunger and death from poisoning . . . I simply picked the latter and prayed for God's forgiveness. Several minutes later, I had a severe stomachache. I poked my fingers deep down in my throat, hoping I could throw up. But because there was nothing in my stomach, the poisonous mushrooms were digested and absorbed very fast. My hands and feet began to tremble. My whole body began to shake. I wrapped myself around a tree and kept praying. If I was going to die, I wanted to die in prayer.

When I woke up, the moon was out. I managed to stand. I was still very hungry, but my stomach pain had gone. "Amen," I murmured to myself. "Amen. Thank you, Lord, for your protection." I was alive when I know I should have been dead.

*Liao:* All three of you survived.

*Zhang:* During the Cultural Revolution, Bishop Liu was taken to somewhere in Haidong for more interrogation. He was beaten many times. His health deteriorated a lot. In 1983, when the Party reversed its policy on religion, we were reunited. The local Religious Affairs Bureau found us a two-bedroom house across the street from the old church. So the three of us moved in there and tried to persuade the residents and the school authorities to give us back our church and the church's property. Bishop Liu cited Party policy in his negotiations and told them, "Even though we are old and feeble, we are not giving in—this is God's church." The residents told him, "To hell with your God."

Next we tried to persuade officials at the local Religious Affairs Bureau. Carrying my aunt on my back, we went to the Dali Prefecture government building, but nobody wanted to talk with us. So I walked out of the building and put my aunt down on the stairs outside. I sat next to her, fasting and staging a sit-in protest.

*Liao:* How old were you then?

*Zhang:* I think I was seventy-five or seventy-six. My aunt was close to ninety. We would come home in the evening and go there again in the morning. My aunt had asthma and could hardly breathe. I told her to stay home, but she refused. "The Lord belongs to all of us, not to you alone, she said." In the 1980s, the road from the old section of Dali to Xiaguan, the prefecture capital, was really bad. Every day, I would get up at the crack of dawn. I would pray first, then sweep the yard and cook breakfast. My aunt had become a nun at the age of twenty-one. She was a beautiful woman and kept herself up really well. She would scold me for being a tomboy. Well, I had to act like a man. I had to do farmwork in the field, raise pigs and chickens. I never had any time to myself. On the first morning of our official sit-in protest, my aunt told me to change into my new clothes: "We are staging a protest in the middle of the street. Don't dress up like a beggar and embarrass the Lord."

I carried her to the bus terminal outside the city's south gate. Two hours later, we were outside the prefecture government building. I laid out a quilt on the ground and had my aunt lie down. I sat next to her and began praying. Soon, we were surrounded by a curious crowd. I told them what had happened. We were there every day. Rain or shine, we didn't care.

All we knew was that there was a large crowd every day. Sometimes the crowd was so thick it was like a human wall. I felt a little uneasy. So, I would stand up, raise the cross above my head, and ask them to disperse. But more people would stop and watch. Some would get close to my aunt and whisper back to the crowd, "The old woman is still breathing. She is mumbling something to herself." I would correct the person by saying, "She's not talking to herself. She's praying." And they would ask, "What is she praying?" And I would repeat her words loudly, "Dear Lord, you put me here to test me in this secular world. Please forgive my sins and correct my thoughts. Please rescue me from the evil forces of this world. Amen."

*Liao:* Did people understand?

*Zhang:* No, they didn't. Many people said we were crazy. Some kindhearted people suggested we give up. "You should think from the government's viewpoint," they'd say. "They have a whole prefecture to run. It's not easy. You should be patriotic and love your country." I didn't argue with them. We stayed outside the government building for twenty-eight days. During the day, I fasted. I would only drink some water. Considering my aunt's poor health, I would feed her some noodle soup around noon. When the sun started to set, I would carry her to the bus terminal and we'd return home in Dali.

As time went by, I found it harder and harder to carry my aunt since I only ate breakfast and fasted all day long. I was losing weight. My legs were weak. So we simply stayed overnight on the street. The building guards and the police tried to kick us out.

We ignored them. Nobody dared to arrest us. We were two old ladies. I'm sure they felt bad for us.

After a while, people on the street became used to our presence. Some would say hi to us when they passed by. There were no longer any crowds. A couple of children would hang out and play with us. But I think our presence must have reflected very badly on the government, because, on the twenty-eighth day, a senior official with two assistants showed up. He stood there for several minutes, then squatted down next to me, "Are you Zhang Yinxian?" "Yes," I said. "And this is my aunt, Li Huazhen." He was a bit sarcastic, and I said, "We don't mean to make trouble for you. We just need a place to live." He was puzzled by my answer and said, "You have a place. Isn't the two-bedroom house big enough for you?" I said quickly, "We are not those childless old people who are on welfare. You can't just throw us a house and shut us up. We want our church back. We need a proper place to worship the Lord." He backed down a little bit and said, "Well, we will return the church assets, eventually. It takes time." I became impatient. "Time? We've been waiting thirty-one years. I'm only seventy years old, so I can still wait, but what about my aunt? She is over ninety. She has many health problems. I don't think she can wait." The official became upset. He raised his voice: "Who do you think you are? You can't threaten the government and tell us what to do. We've been working hard to make it happen for you, but it takes time. You will have to wait at least three or four years more." My aunt was listening, half asleep, and now asked me to help her sit up. She said, "If that's the case, I'm just going to die here, right on the street." I added, "And so will I; the two of us are ready to die right here, in front of the government building." The officer

responded, "Do whatever you want." He was angry, and before
he left, he turned and railed at me, "Are you threatening the
Communist Party?" I said calmly, "All I want is to get the church
back. I won't hold you responsible for our lives."

*Liao:* What happened next?

*Zhang:* A couple of months after that confrontation, we were told we
could have our church back—the old chapel, two rows of houses
around the chapel, and the two courtyard houses. People in the
old section were shocked. They would say, "Those two evil old
women. They were so tough. Even the government caved in."
Well, it's not enough. We've only gotten back one quarter of the
church assets. The two schools across the street used to be part of
the church. That property is as big as three or four football fields.
We'll never get that land back.

*Liao:* The three of you living in this big place; wasn't it like a dream
come true?

*Zhang:* The church doesn't belong to us. We only look after it for the
Lord.

*Liao:* How did you support yourself in those days?

*Zhang:* By then, the other two were old and sick. I raised pigs and
chickens, grew vegetables. We could make ends meet. We were
happy. My aunt died in 1989. She was ninety-three. Bishop Liu
died in 1990 at the age of ninety. They are buried on Cangshan
Mountain. There is a spot next to their graves for me. The day
before Bishop Liu passed away, he told me that he wanted to hold
a Mass in the church, but he had barely put on his robe before
he fell down. I prayed over him, and as he took in his last long
breath, his eyes closed. He was smiling. Dusk was approaching.
I could feel the angels outside, flying into the setting sun. I felt a
gentle breeze.

Now I was alone and felt very sad. I would sometimes catch myself looking for them inside the church, in the courtyard, and in places where they had spent time. One day, I closed my eyes. I felt that they were touching my hands. I was so happy. I woke up and saw it was a dog, licking my hands.

In 1998 things changed. We had a new bishop. A new generation of nuns, such as Sister Tao, arrived. I feel more relaxed now. I will continue to press them to have the government return the remaining church property. Even if we can't get it back, we need to record it in the church history. Future generations should know what happened.

I've been waiting for the Lord to take me. I'm looking forward to reuniting with Bishop Liu and my aunt. While I was not looking, another ten years have passed. I'm going on 101 now. People around here are thirty, forty years younger than I am. What can I do?

*Liao:* What would you like to do?

*Zhang:* I would like to continue to praise the Lord. I would like to continue to make sure that our church gets back our land. I would like to continue . . .

*Chapter 3*

## THE TIBETAN

Bars and nightclubs on Foreigner Street in Dali look different in the daylight without their flattering neon signs and the hypnotic thump thump thump of their music; I imagine a model woken up too early, without her makeup and glamorous outfits. The smell was different, too, in the fresh morning air: body odor and stale marijuana smoke. Beyond were the vegetable vendors, Bai women in their colorful dress calling attention to the fruits and vegetables from their land, their displays smelling earthy and real, leaves unusually lush and thick. I stopped to admire the bok choy and, out of mischief, asked if it was genetically engineered. The Bai woman looked at me through narrowed eyes, smiled toothlessly, and scolded: "You damn ghost from Sichuan."

At a little after nine o'clock on August 3, 2009, I turned right on Renmin Avenue into a small stone-paved lane, following the directional signs for "The Catholic Church." The door to one courtyard was open, and, from the lane, the "church" within appeared at first glance no different from any of the other old residential houses in the neighborhood. Though its eaves were carved with the birds and animals of Bai legends, reaching into the sky was a steeple topped by a cross painted gold. Inside, the ceiling arched several stories high, and the building took the shape of a butterfly, its wings stretched ready for flight.

Sunday Mass had just started as I slipped quietly through the waves of singing from the hundred or so parishioners and eased along a pew to join my friend Kun Peng. Not knowing how to sing hymns, I hummed the melody. At the altar, against the background of four big Chinese characters proclaiming God Is Love, a middle-aged priest and two young acolytes were immersed in an ancient ceremony. "For Jesus had known from the beginning which of them did not believe and who would betray him," the priest intoned. I felt a little self-conscious about my presence in the church, a nonbeliever here to observe the behavior of believers. I knew the passage the priest was reading and hoped they did not think the betrayer was me.

The service had a rhythm of rising and falling, like the wash of the tide against a beach: standing to sing the hymn, sitting to hear the sermon, kneeling to pray, standing again to sing another hymn. Kun Peng had told me that with the repetition of each act, the heart became purer, more pious and more passionate. We all stood again when the organ began to play, and the congregation made a line in the aisle to receive Holy Communion, the wafer and wine that were the body and blood of Christ.

I was not alone in remaining seated; there was a smattering of other nonbelievers here out of curiosity or simply to enjoy the music. By eleven o'clock, the Mass was over, and Kun Peng took me to see the monastery next door. High walls divided the views of two traditional Bai-style courtyard houses, where plants and flowers grew in the garden, lush and in full bloom. The houses looked dilapidated. Nuns and monks shuffled in and out, some in robes, others not, going about their Sunday business. Among them was a young man who said he was twenty-four, Tibetan, Catholic, and a seminarian. Like most Chinese, I was under the impression that every Tibetan was a devout follower of Tibetan Buddhism.

Jia Bo-er was squatting under the eaves, washing his robe in a basin, his shiny, black, curly hair bobbing up and down in the sun as he pressed and kneaded the black cloth. He said his Christian name was Gabriel, and when he was done with his washing, we found some shade to talk. He said he was from Shangri-La:

*Liao Yiwu:* Shangri-La? Isn't that the famous paradise described in James Hilton's novel *Lost Horizon?*

*Jia Bo-er:* Yes, yes. Most of my friends have read the novel. It was written in 1933, I think. The paradise that Hilton described in the book was supposed to be in the Cizhong region, Diqing Prefecture, part of Yunnan province. In the 1990s, leaders of the prefecture officially certified that our village was the "lost Shangri-La." I think it was a stunt to attract tourists. I'm quite proud that my hometown is so well known.

Generations of my family have lived in the Cizhong area. In the old days, we were all Buddhists. About two hundred years ago, soldiers from the Lamaseries constantly engaged in fights against the Chinese troops. The war lasted many years and left many villages in poverty and chaos. Old folks would tell me that in the war-torn region, people died all the time. In the mid-nineteenth century, several priests with a Catholic organization called Foreign Missions of Paris arrived. They changed the lives of many ordinary people.

*Liao:* Are there more Buddhists or Christians in the Cizhong area?

*Jia:* I think it's half and half. We all live in the same village, share the same skin color, wear similar goatskin coats, and herd goats and farm together. So it's quite harmonious. When we get together for dinner with our friends or neighbors, they chant their Buddhist sutras and we say our prayers to seek God's blessing. Then we toast each other with liquor. Occasionally, we would take off our necklaces and compare whose pendants are prettier, the cross or the miniatures of Buddha. You have probably read

about the meeting between Pope John Paul II and the Dalai
Lama? They praised each other warmly during their meeting.
It is good to promote interfaith harmony, don't you think? Four
generations of my family have been Christians. I've been a
Christian all my life.

*Liao:* Your name doesn't sound Tibetan.

*Jia:* You are right. It's a Western name. I was baptized in a church.
The priest named me "Gabriel." Gabriel is one of God's angels,
and the name means "man of God." As you know, we Tibetans
name our children quite spontaneously. A father is supposed to
come up with a name immediately upon the birth of his child. Many
times, he gets his inspiration from whatever he sees first when he
steps outside the house. If it's a Kalsang flower blooming on the
grassland, he will name his baby girl Kal Sang, or Ge Sang. If it's a
windy morning, he's very likely to name his baby boy Anil, which
means "wind" or "air." I like my biblical name a lot.

*Liao:* Where were you baptized?

*Jia:* In the Cizhong church, which was built by French missionaries
about 150 years ago.

*Liao:* Is it the oldest church in Yunnan province?

*Jia:* Probably. When you are in the valley area, you can see from
a distance its Western-style steeple against the snow-covered
mountain peaks, surrounded by Buddhist temples. The Lancang
River flows by and then curves around the villages there. Old
folks in my village used to say that Cizhong was a borderland
for Christian missionaries. From the mid-nineteenth to the early
twentieth centuries, missionaries hoped that the gospel would
filter into Tibet, but the lamas didn't like religious competition
and many priests were killed. The Kashag, or the governing
council of Tibet, placed thousands of troops at key mountain
passes to prevent outsiders from entering Tibet. It didn't matter

whether you were a Han or a Westerner, and it didn't matter if you carried a gun or a Bible. The troops would arrest you or kill you. Many people went and never returned. In the end, the missionaries established bases in Cizhong from which to serve the Tibetan villages.

*Liao:* Are there many Christians in Tibet?

*Jia:* No. I think there are only about seven hundred or so. In Cizhong, the Catholic missionaries were the first to arrive, but as travel has become easier the Protestant churches have also been expanding. In recent years, Cizhong has become a popular destination for tourists from France, America, Britain, Canada, Australia, Sweden, and New Zealand. On their way to climb the Meili Snow Mountain, many stop and worship at the Cizhong church.

*Liao:* Have you heard any stories about early Western missionaries in the region?

*Jia:* Yes. I've seen their tombstones. Some of them were damaged during the Cultural Revolution, but now they have been restored and are protected. I've also seen trees planted by foreign missionaries at the beginning of the last century. The missionaries picked mountain slopes that faced the sun to plant grapes. We call them "rose honey." They have a strong, thick, and sweet taste. They are part of an ancient variety in France. The missionaries brought winemaking techniques to the region.

*Liao:* I have tasted rose-honey wine. It is red and mild.

*Jia:* It doesn't scratch your throat like barley wine does. The French missionaries originally intended it just for Holy Communion. But after they had settled in our village and built a church there, people easily overcame cultural difference and treated them like family. The Tibetans would offer highland barley wine to their French friends, who offered their red rose-honey wine in return.

Tibetan traders and farmers would go to the church not to pray or sing hymns—they were still Buddhists—but to visit their French friends and drink wine with them. I'm told that sometimes a local farmer would enjoy too many glasses of wine and the priests would find him a bed to sleep it off.

During harvest seasons, the French priests would bring their wine to the barley field and help farmers with harvesting and planting. They also tried to teach them how to sing hymns. You know, Tibetans are good at bellowing out loud mountain tunes. They open their mouths and howl. The priest would stop them, saying: "Amen; God bless your voice. But you don't have to howl. God is not deaf. He can hear you." The French priests made lots of adjustments to the hymns. Nowadays, psalms are sung with Tibetan highland melodies. Sunday Mass will sometimes feature a dance around a bonfire. Christmas is celebrated with dancing around bonfires.

Relations between local Tibetans and foreign missionaries have not always been easy though. We Tibetans suffered deeply, sometimes ravaged by war, other times by pandemics, at times both war and pandemics.

I was told that in my great-great-grandfather's time, the region was hit by a severe drought. For several consecutive years, there was no rain or snow. The riverbed lay exposed. Goats and cattle died of starvation because there was no grass to feed them. Crops withered to sticks. People's lives were in danger. The lamas chanted and prayed for rain. It didn't help. People burned incense to local gods and deities. Nothing. Some Tibetans began to vent their frustrations on the foreign missionaries. Some claimed that Tibetans had offended their ancestors because they had invited foreigners to their villages and allowed them to change their faith.

In one area, local villagers surrounded a church and captured the lone priest. They tied him up and carried him up to the mountains where they planned to sacrifice him to their ancestors. When the knife fell on the priest's neck, his head turned into a piece of blue rock. From his neck spurted not blood but milk, which streamed down the mountain and into the village. Everyone hastened out. They jumped into the stream to drink the nurturing liquid. Just like that, the blighted land was rejuvenated. People were grateful and carried the priest's body down the mountain and buried him at the back of his church. Ever since, they pray in front of the priest's tomb to seek God's protection when disaster hits.

*Liao:* History and legends are only separated by a thin wall. Sometimes, it's okay to climb over.

*Jia:* Let me share with you another one, "The story of the golden needles." Bubonic plague and cholera struck our region many decades ago. A large swath of the population died. Survivors escaped to other places. Village after village became empty. Even the Han and Tibetan troops had to stop their protracted war against each other. There was silence everywhere. Fortunately, the missionaries arrived with many golden needles. It was vaccine for the plague, and they had pills for cholera. Some recovered fast, some more slowly, but soon everyone became better.

*Liao:* I've heard many stories about how Western missionaries saved lives through their medical services. They played a big role in stopping the spread of epidemics in many parts of China.

*Jia:* As a child, I remember seeing adults sitting around a bonfire at night. After downing shots of liquor, they would start telling such stories, but I was too young to remember them all. My parents had seven children; several of my siblings have much better memories than I.

*Liao:* Seven children?

*Jia:* I have three elder sisters and three younger brothers. I'm in the middle, but the eldest son. I'm very lucky they sent me to Chengdu to study theology. I've always been attracted to the church. Whatever the Lord wants me to do, I obey his plan.

But sometimes I'm not as determined as I should be. Many of my elders, such as Sister Tao and Father Ding, are much more devoted. Many of my fellow seminarians renew their commitment vows every three years. Three times three is nine. After nine years, they will make a final vow to remain celibate and serve the Lord for the rest of their lives. I'm still hesitating and pondering my future. I'm not as devoted as my elders.

*Liao:* You are only twenty-four. Are you still hesitant about your future with the church because you want to get married?

*Jia:* No. I'm not thinking about the issue now.

*Liao:* Are you planning to go back to Cizhong after seminary?

*Jia:* No.

*Liao:* Why not? Cizhong is your hometown and it's a great place.

*Jia:* I belong to the church. I will go wherever the church sends me. The Bible says that Jesus left his hometown and wandered around the world for many years. So since I've already left, I'm not going back. I'm ready to travel the country and serve God.

*Liao:* The Catholic Church holds you to the rule of celibacy. The Protestant churches are different.

*Jia:* Some people think the Catholics are more conservative. It might be true. That's why the secular government feels more threatened by the Catholics.

*Liao:* Really?

*Jia:* Let me give you an example. There's a poster at the entrance about a missing person who lived more than two thousand years ago. It says: "Jesus from Nazareth, 1.80 meters tall, with brown curly hair, bright piercing eyes brimming with vigor, his voice sonorous and forceful. He doesn't bow to evil forces and he detests hypocrisies. God is the path. He represents truth and life. If you find Him, please follow Him."

*Liao:* Do you pledge loyalty to the Vatican?

*Jia:* Not really. Bishops and priests who have relations with the Vatican are being monitored closely by the government. They try very hard to block any contacts with the Vatican. The Communist Party has planted many of its people inside the church. The government constantly reminds the clergy not to stray or do anything to violate the Party policy. Before any kind of large-scale Mass, the government has to approve the contents of the sermon.

*Liao:* Do you bow to evil forces?

*Jia:* I have not been tested yet.

*Liao:* What about your parents?

*Jia:* They went through the destructive Cultural Revolution. The only thing they mentioned was that they didn't give up on God. They prayed secretly. They don't want to dwell too much on the past. I think most Catholics in China feel the same way.

*Chapter 4*

## THE ELDER (I)

In the course of my research I came across a copy of Wu Yongsheng's *The History of Christianity in Dali*, which outlines the work of early missionaries in southwest China. I was determined to talk to the author about the past and present spread of the Christian religion.

The Old City Protestant Church, or "Fuyintang," was built in 1905. Occupying more than three hundred square meters, Fuyintang is architecturally mixed—Bai ethnic residential meets European gothic. Its facade is exposed stone, and a cross painted in red stands prominently atop a traditional Chinese roof tower that resembles an eagle flapping in flight. Old courtyard houses and Bai buildings in the vicinity are dwarfed by its presence.

The chapel was empty when I called on the afternoon of August 11, 2009, with my monk friend Ze Yu. We stepped out and turned into a small quiet lane near the chapel. Based on the address provided by the church staff, we knocked on the door of a small courtyard house. An elderly lady with gray hair popped her head out, looking stern and annoyed. When she heard we were friends of the church, she mulled it over for a few seconds and led us to a spartanly furnished house, inside of which were hung crosses and scrolls of Bible proverbs and a family portrait I took to be of Wu and his wife, Zhang Fengxiang (the gray-haired lady), and their offspring—some twenty in total.

Wu Yongsheng was born in 1924. An elder at the Dali Old City Protestant Church, he was highly respected in the Christian community. Three months before our visit, he had a stroke and fell. He received timely treatment and, though his movement was impaired and he walked with a cane, had retained all his faculties and was articulate, his mind lucid. He presented me with a copy of the Book of Psalms. I accepted it, saying that I would "study up on it." Wu corrected me, saying, "You should use it as a mirror to confess your sins and reform." He urged monk Ze to abdicate his pursuit of enlightenment through Buddha and look to Jesus for salvation. Ze responded with a smile.

During our interview, Wu was guarded, even evasive, when I asked about his views on the past political campaigns, though the reason for his reluctance to discuss such questions became clear toward the end of our visit.

*Wu Yongsheng:* I was born in the provincial capital of Kunming. In 1937, when I was finishing up elementary school, my mother's younger brother returned to Kunming from Dali and told me to quit school. "The whole country is in chaos," he said. "Disasters are imminent. What's the point of attending school?" This uncle asked me to apprentice with him and become a carpenter. Even though the war [with Japan] had not officially started, you could feel it. There were sirens all the time. Food prices went up dramatically and people hoarded goods. Our family lived in constant fear. My uncle's offer made my parents happy, and I returned with him to Dali on an old-style bus that carried both people and merchandise. We spent four days on a road that was paved with rocks as big as potatoes. It was such a bumpy ride. I felt like my whole body was falling apart. Nowadays, when you come from Kunming, it takes half a day.

*Liao Yiwu:* Did your uncle have his own business in Dali?

*Wu:* Yes. He ran his own shop in Dali's old section. As an apprentice, at first I only helped him with some simple errands. He was a Christian and knew many foreign missionaries in town. Each time they needed some work done, they would look for him. He treated me as his own child and took me to Sunday services every week. Soon, I learned the Bible and knew how to sing hymns. In 1940, an American couple arrived in Dali.

*Liao:* Do you remember their names?

*Wu:* Let me see . . . Mr. and Mrs. Harold Taylor. They rented a small courtyard house on Foreigner Street. They put up a sign on their door. It said "The Christian Church." They asked us to renovate the house. During the renovation, we lived on the second floor. The Taylors would leave the house in the morning and come back late at night. They treated us very nicely. They requested that we say a prayer or read the Bible before starting work every day. We followed their advice. By June 1941, I felt inspired by God and was baptized. I was seventeen.

On the day of my baptism, my uncle woke me up at dawn. "It's the day of your rebirth today," my uncle said. The old city wall was still in good shape back then, and you could see all of the four tower gates from the town center. We went through the western gate and waited near a stream that poured down from Cangshan Mountain. A water mill had been built there to grind grain. The mill had two big wooden wheels and operated day and night. In the 1940s, the water mill was a novelty. Reverend Taylor was only in his thirties and liked technology. He thought the stream at the mill an appropriate place to baptize me. He had me step into a pond on the right side of the waterwheel and recited some verses.

His big hands held my small thin body. Slowly, he submerged me in the water, from head to toe. I kept my eyes open and could see the top of the city wall, Cangshan Mountain, and then the white clouds and blue sky. I thought I would see my creator residing high up in heaven but was content to feel surrounded by beautiful white clouds.

*Liao:* It must have been a wonderful feeling.

*Wu:* After the ceremony, Reverend Taylor held my hands and said in his broken Chinese: "Brother Wu, thanks for taking over." I didn't understand what he meant until the Taylors had to leave Dali. The Japanese troops had moved in from Myanmar and occupied the nearby city of Tengchong. They were bombing Kunming and Xiaguan. Many Americans decided to leave.

*Liao:* Were there a lot of foreigners in Dali?

*Wu:* Quite a lot. Some didn't stay long though. They just came and went.

*Liao:* Were the Taylors well known in the region?

*Wu:* Not really. They stayed in Dali for no more than two years. They built a small church and had a limited number of followers. The most famous missionary couple was Mr. and Mrs. Liang Xisheng. Their English names were, let me see, Mr. and Mrs. William Allen. They were very well known in the region. They served in the Dali region for more than ten years and were known for their generosity, both material and spiritual. Unlike the Taylors, they were successful and had gathered a large following. Many high school students took English lessons from them at home. One night, as Mrs. Allen was saying her nightly prayers, she suddenly noticed a man's foot sticking out from under her bed—one of her former students had snuck into their house to steal food. Before he had time to run away, Mrs. Allen walked in. He hid under her bed, hoping to escape after she fell asleep. Mrs. Allen jumped up and screamed with fear. Scared by the noise, the thief crawled in farther. Reverend Allen rushed in from the living room. He bent down, trying to persuade the thief to come out by saying, "You don't have to worry. We are not reporting you to the police. I know your family is poor. Just come out and take whatever you want. I don't care." The thief started crying and promised to crawl out if Reverend Allen would step away from the bed. Meanwhile, Mrs. Allen said, "My dear, I will pray for you. I will ask the Lord to forgive your sins." The thief answered, "No thanks, I don't need you to pray for me. I'm not a Christian." After he finally got out, the thief saw something shining in Reverend Allen's hand. Thinking it was a weapon, the thief pulled out his knife and stabbed at Reverend Allen's thigh. It turned out Reverend Allen was holding a glass of water for the thief. The stabbing shocked Mrs. Allen, who ran out and screamed, "Help, Help." The neighbors heard commotion and helped catch the thief.

*Liao:* What a story. What happened to the thief?

*Wu:* The next day, Reverend Allen went to the police station and bailed the thief out. He knew the poor kid was driven to burglary because of poverty. He never pressed any charges. For a while, it was big news here and spread fast in the region. People were really moved by their generosity. When people saw Reverend Allen on the street, they addressed him as a "saint." He would wave his hands and reply in his Dali dialect, "I don't deserve that honor. I'm merely doing the Lord's work."

Since ancient times, Dali has been fertile ground for all types of religion. Gods and deities fill every inch of the land here. Buddhism and Islam were already here when Christianity arrived, but it spread fast because we have had many wonderful Christians like Rev. Allen, who, through their behavior, demonstrated the benevolence of God.

*Liao:* Do you consider yourself one of them?

*Wu:* I'm just an ordinary Christian. I was a carpenter, nothing worth mentioning. Anyway, after Japan bombed Pearl Harbor, the United States entered the war. Some Westerners working in the Japanese-occupied territories were arrested and murdered. Many were forced to escape south. A lot of them came to Dali. The China Inland Mission had established a Christian hospital in Henan province around 1906, and the hospital moved to Dali around that time.

*Liao:* I read about the China Inland Mission, a British missionary organization that was founded in London in 1865 by James Hudson Taylor. From your own book, I learned that Reverend Taylor and sixteen other missionaries arrived in Shanghai in 1866. They were probably among the earliest Christian foreign missionaries in China.

*Wu:* Probably.

*Liao:* Please, go on with your story.

*Wu:* In 1942 the Japanese troops moved in from Myanmar. Cities like Wanding, Tengchong, and Baoshan fell one after another. Kunming and Xiaguang were frequently bombed. The Christian hospital was open to all people. Doctors were busy treating wounded civilians and soldiers. There was an outbreak of cholera. It was really busy there. I did carpentry work for the hospital and became a regular employee. I became interested in medicine, took classes, and became a doctor at the hospital and stayed there until I retired in 1988.

*Liao:* Doesn't that rather oversimplify your life in the past sixty some years?

*Wu:* I don't want to dwell on the past. Besides, after I had my stroke, my memory is no longer good. Our Christian hospital was the best in the whole southwestern region. We helped thousands of patients.

I still remember the names of many missionaries. People like De Meichun (Jessie McDonald), Bao Wenlian (Frances Powell), Shi Airen (M. E. Scott) and Ma Guangqi (Doris M. L. Madden) had moved to Dali from Henan province at the end of 1941. They devoted their lives to serving the people here. But when the Communist troops came, they forced all foreign missionaries to leave. I still remember the date, May 4, 1951, when the troops took over the hospital. They reviewed the asset inventories, then ordered our hospital president, Jessie McDonald, to sign over all the hospital's assets. Then they kicked her out.

*Liao:* Were you condemned?

*Wu:* Comparatively speaking, the attacks against me were minimal. After all, I was only a staff member at the hospital. At that time, we had about fifty staff members; only ten of us were Christians.

*Liao:* Did you attend public denunciation meetings?

*Wu:* I wasn't singled out, but we had to attend many political study sessions.

*Liao:* Did they question your close relations with foreign missionaries?

*Wu:* The foreign missionaries had all left. There was nothing left to question. I did have to write many confessions. I've written hundreds of confessions in my life.

*Liao:* Did they allow people to attend church services?

*Wu:* We were allowed at the beginning. Then all religious activities were banned. Many people were too scared to go. Some attended services at the beginning until they openly renounced their beliefs. I persisted throughout. In the end, I simply prayed at home.

*Liao:* Did it feel strange to attend Communist study sessions during the day and pray to God at home in the evenings?

*Wu:* I would do whatever the authorities wanted me to do at work. However, secular politics couldn't replace spiritual pursuits.

*Liao:* In the 1950s, Reverend Wu Yaozong in Beijing established the Three-Self Patriotic Church, which was then endorsed by the government. Did you support the Three-Self principles?

*Wu:* When the Westerners left, the churches already followed the principles of self-governance, self-propagation and self-support. In Dali, we also established the Three-Self Patriotic Committee. Reverend Duan Liben was the director. I supported the tenets laid out in the Bible.

*Liao:* Did you openly state that position in the Mao era?

*Wu:* Oh, I wouldn't dare. In 1952 the Dali United Front Department ordered Christian churches of different denominations to merge. We had the Catholic Church, the Episcopalian Church, and the Old City Church. We held services together until the political campaigns became really bad. The revolutionary masses had been mobilized to attack Christians. The slogan was "hurting their flesh to change their souls." As a result, people left the church in droves. In the end, the only open Christians in Dali were Reverend Hou Wuling and his wife, Li Quanben, and Yang Fengzhen . . .

*Liao:* What happened to them?

*Wu:* They all died tragically. Reverend Hou Wuling had been publicly denounced several times. He died during a public study session, an aneurism . . . but please, let's not talk about him. It breaks my heart to even think about it.

Before the Cultural Revolution ended, all open religious activities had been banned. Churches and church assets had been seized. Only in silence could people pray and read Scripture. It was a treat just to move our lips and shape the name of God.

I couldn't bring myself to openly boycott the government policies. I didn't dare reveal my true faith in public. When I realized that I couldn't do it, I asked God for forgiveness. Thanks to the merciful Lord, I was able to survive the political campaigns of the 1950s.

*Liao:* Did you suffer during the Cultural Revolution?

*Wu:* The Red Guards wanted to sweep away all sorts of "snakes and demons." My wife and I couldn't escape. Our home was ransacked; we were interrogated. They put dunce caps on us and paraded us through the streets. They burned our precious collections of biblical books. Oh, so sad . . . but the past is like passing clouds. I just let it go.

*[Zhang Fengxiang, seeing how affected her husband was, intervened at this point in the interview and offered to continue his story. "The past is too traumatic for my husband," she said. "He doesn't want to revisit it, especially after his stroke."]*

*Zhang Fengxiang:* I was born into a poor family in 1933 in the city of Chuxiong, Yunnan province. There was a Bethel Church near my home. When I was five, I began joining many children in the neighborhood to attend free classes at the church. Our teachers were foreigners with blue eyes and big noses. They smiled all the time and were very patient. They taught us how to read and write in English. Then we learned to pray and sing hymns. A few years later, we started learning Bible stories. I loved going to the classes because the teachers would distribute candies and toys to us if we came up with the right answers to their questions. Under their influence, I became a Christian and was baptized at the age of fifteen. In 1950 I was enrolled in a nursing school affiliated with the Christian hospital in Dali and became a nurse after graduation. In 1953, when I was twenty, I married Wu Yongsheng in a local church. We both worked at the same hospital.

At the beginning of the Cultural Revolution, we became the primary targets at the hospital. We suffered all sorts of tortures. The Maoist rebels accused us of being spies. They gathered all of us in front of our church, beating drums and gongs, and sang revolutionary songs. They held a public denunciation meeting there. First they piled up all the biblical books and documents, and then they set them on fire. They cheered and danced. Several Christians, including my husband and I, were forced to bend down at a ninety-degree angle by the fire.

They were still not satisfied. They smashed the windows, the pews, the bookshelves, the furniture, old scrolls of paintings, and even the pipe organ that was brought there by Western missionaries. You know, there used to be a gigantic bell installed inside the church's top tower. They took it down and tried to break it but couldn't make a single crack. In the end, they took it away. Nobody knows where it is now. Such a shame. The bell was made in London and transported to Dali in 1905.

They were thorough. Nothing was left. One of them thought that because we were spies we might have hidden a telegraph machine or weapons. My husband insisted we were not spies. But their leader wouldn't listen. "When those imperialists left, they planted you here. They assigned you special tasks. You'd better confess if you want lenient treatment." I stepped up and explained on behalf of my husband, "We are not allowed to hide anything

illegal in the church. It is a holy place." They scolded me for
being as stubborn as granite. They got hold of some shovels and
electric drills. Within a few hours, they destroyed the floor and
had dug a big hole in the middle of the chapel.

*Liao:* They must have seen too many spy movies.

*Zhang:* Later, the church was occupied by a dozen or so local
residents who decided to live there. The chapel was converted
into workshops for blacksmiths, stove makers, pottery makers,
and carpenters. We were detained and tortured. Each time we
were released, we went back to work at the hospital and continued
to take care of patients. One day, a group of peasants put up a
poster saying "Thank you." The poster was next to a bunch of
slogans: "Smash the dog heads of Wu Yongsheng and Zhang
Fengxiang."

We tried to make the best of a bad situation. We accepted the
humiliation without resistance.

My husband mentioned Reverend Duan Liben, who headed
the local Three-Self Patriotic Committee. In 1956 he traveled
to Beijing for a national conference on reforming the Christian
churches in China. In July 1966 the local government ordered
all the local Catholic and Protestant leaders to attend a "religious
conference." It turned out to be a trap. For forty days they were
detained for interrogation. Then, Reverend Duan was sent to
the countryside to "reform his thinking through hard labor."
He suffered a lot, more than ordinary Christians like us. He's no
longer with us.

In 1980 the United Front Department notified us that we could
hold Sunday services. The worshipping service had been banned
for more than two decades. They did not return many of the
church's assets, and we doubt they ever will.

*Chapter 5*

## THE EPISCOPALIAN

In 1937, after Japan invaded China, Cai Yongchun and Wu Shengde, two professors from Huazhong University in the central city of Wuhan, relocated to Dali and founded the Dali Episcopalian Church. In 1943 the two founders received funding from the dioceses in Shanghai and bought twenty buildings and houses on one and a half acres of land. They converted the properties into a chapel, an orphanage, and an elementary school to accelerate the spread of the gospel. In 1948 Hou Wuling, a young priest, took over the church. In 1964, during a political study session, Reverend Hou took out a cross hidden in his breast pocket and slipped to the ground. He died of an aneurism.

Wu Yongsheng, *The History of Christianity in Dali*

Who was this young priest, Hou Wuling? His mention in Wu Yongsheng's book was so brief that it didn't shed much light on the man's life or the circumstances surrounding his death. How could such a religious leader, for he clearly was that, pass like a meteor, flashing momentarily and then disappearing with scarcely a trace? What happened to him under Communism? What prompted him to bring out the hidden cross at that political study session? I was intrigued; I like a good mystery. I began by examining existing church records but could find nothing about Hou.

In Wu's book, I also found a brief mention that when the government reversed its verdict against Hou, Wu was responsible for reaching out to Hou's family. Wu had told me that Hou headed the local Episcopalian church in Dali but refused to give me further details. Was he dodging a political landmine?

I contacted Kun Peng, who seemed to know everyone who mattered. I needed more information and hoped Kun could point me in the right direction. I particularly wanted to find Hou's family members. Kun called me back a few days later. He hadn't managed to trace Hou's daughter but found three other elderly Christians who might know something about Hou's life. I interviewed all of them and obtained some details.

Hou did take charge of the Dali Episcopal Church in 1948, a time when the country was embroiled in civil war. He was responsible for the assets that the church had accumulated over the years but was mainly concerned with ministering to the thousands of followers who lived in constant fear of the war. He was in his prime and diligent in his duties. Wu remembered that Hou had tried to keep the church neutral in the war between the Communists and the ruling Nationalists and divorced from politics after Mao Zedong's victory in 1949. But the new Communist government considered foreign missionaries as hostile forces. Religious networks of all faiths crumbled. Christians renounced their faith at public meetings as "a shameful chapter" in their lives. Hou was devastated by the turn of events. His refusal to renounce his faith made him a political target. At a conference held by the United Front Department, one official confronted Hou: "Are you trying to challenge the power of the revolutionary masses?" He remained silent; his answer lay in his actions—he continued to follow the Lord and was guardian of his church. He was nicknamed "The Silent Lamb."

With each successive political campaign, Communist officials made him a target. In 1953 the government wanted him to surrender the Huiyu Elementary School, which had been founded and operated by the Dali Episcopal Church. Officials proposed changing its name to Dali No. 2 Elementary School. Hou refused to let government officials enter the school. They countered by sending him a bill for the school's utility fees and repair costs. With all funding sources cut off under the new regime, Hou couldn't pay, so he disconnected the electricity and told students: "Our hearts are open and lit by truth; we don't need electric lights."

While Hou was praying by candlelight in the school's chapel, local militiamen broke in and took him away. They accused him of sabotaging school facilities and engaging in counterrevolutionary actions. After the government raided his church and reviewed his finances, they charged him with counterrevolutionary corruption. Soon after that, the government brought another charge against him—raping underage female orphans. With one accusation after another directed at him, Hou was arrested and held for a year, but there was insufficient evidence for a conviction, so he was released.

As Hou stood watch over his flock, he remained in conflict with the Party. One day a Christian woman named Li Huijun showed up at his door with her ten-year-old daughter. They were escaping from her rural village, where her family had been persecuted as members of the "evil landlord class." Hou and his wife took them in. A few months later, Li's daughter, who had tuberculosis, died. Subsequently, the street committee noticed Li's presence in the church and, having ascertained her family background, sent her back to her village. Li escaped again. The local militiamen hunted her down and brought her back. In 1954 she ran away for the third time and hid in the church. Her captors followed her to Dali. She was found in a room next to the church library. Li had hanged herself.

In the same year, Hou was asked to support and join the newly formed Three-Self Patriotic Church. He refused, calling it "collective surrender." Local progovernment religious leaders held a conference and "unanimously" voted that he be stripped of his title and barred from participating in any religious activities. In 1957 he was labeled a Rightist. In 1958 the local government in Dali officially seized the Dali Episcopal Church land and converted it into a chemical plant. Hou was threatened with imprisonment if he refused to move out. He was assigned a bed in a dorm for factory workers. His wife and a daughter went back to Chengdu to live with her parents.

Hou was a regular at public denunciations, which continued even as famine swept China in 1959. A Christian survivor told me that people were too weak to beat up class enemies, so instead, the masses would pinch and bite them. He remembered seeing Hou covered with bruises.

In 1963 the government under President Liu Shaoqi adopted a series of policies to curb Mao's radical industrialization and nationalization programs and help alleviate the famine situation. Mao retreated. Persecution of Christians abated, and there was more food. In 1964 Mao countered with his "Socialist Education Campaign," and Hou was called to attend a weeklong political study session with forty other Rightists and counterrevolutionaries at a segregated building guarded by soldiers. He was forced to answer question after question until he simply stopped talking and dropped to the ground, dead. There is no official record on the specifics of his death, and those in attendance suffered collective amnesia. All I have to go on are the lines from Wu's book: that Hou took out his cross, slipped to the ground, and died of an aneurism. The interrogations, public denunciation meetings, and political study sessions were over for him.

We know Hou's body was cremated several hours after he died. No autopsy was performed. Several days later, Hou's wife arrived from Chengdu and took an urn of his ashes home. According to Mr. Wu, she never dared ask how her husband had died. Maybe it was good that he had died before the Cultural Revolution, Wu said.

In 1980 the United Front Department of Dali issued a notice officially exonerating Hou of any wrongdoing. Wu accepted the notice on behalf of the Hou family and then mailed it to Hou Mei-en, the daughter in Chengdu. He is certain that Hou's wife and daughter are still alive, though he has heard nothing from them in thirty years. I asked if the government had compensated the family for its suffering, and Wu shook his head, "Not a single penny." Church assets were sold off by the government to private developers. The state-run chemical plant built on the church property went bankrupt and was closed. The land is now occupied by the Internal Medicine Department of Dali's No. 2 People's Hospital.

*Chapter 6*

## THE CANCER PATIENT

Stripes of light from the setting sun occupied a corner of Li Linshan's tiny courtyard. As Li was talking, he massaged a large lump of flour dough to make shells for dumplings. His pale face turned crimson from the effort; sweat beaded his forehead. I had heard he was a singer and urged him to give me some local Shanxi opera tunes. He straightened his back and took a deep breath, exhaled. He said the opera required that the singer howl in a higher register but he no longer had the strength and that the best he'd be able to manage would be a lower octave. "I might sound like a woman," he warned. I really liked his version; I thought it mixed in some styles of hymn singing. I applauded enthusiastically.

When the steamy dumplings were put on a low table in the courtyard, we sat and Li led a prayer of thanks, which went on for some time. "Today is Praying for World Peace Day. Lord, you have brought Brother Kun Peng and Mr. Liao over to listen to my humble life story. They are prominent intellectuals but are willing to be friends with me. I thank you for your blessing and hope you bless them with good health . . ." Heads were bowed in silence around the table. I watched the dumplings grow cold. Having experienced the famine of the 1960s, I never refuse food and am somewhat of a glutton, but I ate slowly and smiled throughout the meal. I smiled when we finished our interview and shook hands to bid our good-byes. I smiled for about half a mile along the road. I didn't want to smile, and my face hurt from faking it; I had been in a house of great suffering.

A gathering thunderstorm finally broke, with torrents of rain and strong winds, but soon the moon rose, and the clearing clouds looked like dangling shreds of wet mountain moss against the lunar light.

I first heard of Li Linshan from my friend Kun Peng in the spring of 2009. Kun urged me to visit Li immediately. "Otherwise, it will be too late," he said.

Arrangements were made, and at about noon on August 16 I set out along a narrow muddy path through a vast expanse of grassland. I could see cows and packs of dogs to the far left of me in the meadow. As I approached the foot of a mountain, I heard the booming of a distant thunderstorm. Clouds as big as ships floated overhead. There had been a big storm the night before, and my dreams had been filled with disturbing images of rising waters that submerged the town and reached a mountain peak, leaving me the only survivor, jumping from mountaintop to mountaintop like a monkey.

Li lived in the old section of Dali, and Kun Peng met me at Renmin Avenue to guide me the rest of the way, down narrow alleyways, turning left and right until we reached Guangwu Street, where we stopped outside a doorway, horizontal red poster atop the faded wooden doorframe proclaiming in four prominent Chinese characters: The Blessings of God.

Kun shouted for Li from the street. A tanned woman opened the door. She was Li's current wife. They had been married for five years. Kun led me to the middle of the tiny courtyard and introduced me to Li, who was squatting in a corner, a kitchen knife in each hand. "So nice to meet you," Li said. "Sorry, I can't shake hands; I'm making dumplings for you." He went back to his chopping and slicing, and Kun took my arm, whispering, "Brother Li is little more than a bag of bones." Surprised by Kun's blunt remarks, I said, "He's a little thin, but he looks quite energetic." Li heard me and laughed. "I'm energetic because it's a special day today. I'm very excited about your visit. That's why I'm making dumplings. This is the first time I've cooked since I became ill. Who knows, it could also be my last." Li said he was using a traditional recipe from his native Shanxi province. "I have to cut the meat and vegetables very finely. I want to treat you to an authentic Shanxi dumpling feast." Li was soon done, and as he wiped his hands on an old cloth, we began our talk:

*Liao Yiwu:* How did you get sick?

*Li Linshan:* Hmm . . . actually, I don't know. I think I've always been sick. I was born in 1963, at the tail end of the three-year famine. While she was pregnant, my mother couldn't get enough to eat in the city. She returned to her native village in Shanxi province. According to my grandma, when I was born, I looked like a tiny pussycat, clutching myself, too weak to even cry. My parents didn't think I would survive and had decided to abandon me, but my grandma stopped them. She said, "He's breathing. If we wrap him up near the fire, we can probably warm him up and save him." My father sighed and said, "We haven't been able to feed ourselves for three years. How are you going to be able to raise this kid? Besides, he doesn't seem to have the lungs for singing."

*Liao:* Your parents were singers?

*Li:* They were professional singers with a local Chinese opera group. They were quite well known in Luozi opera. My parents performed with the opera group for several years, but the times were hard so they returned to their home village in Danshan Township. They thought farming would provide a stable income, but they had never been lucky. A major source of their misery was my health. I've been constantly tortured with all sorts of illnesses. But poor people can't afford a doctor.

*Liao:* And now?

*Li:* I have what the doctor calls "carcinoma gastric cardia." The cancer is here, where my throat meets my stomach. When the doctor diagnosed it in 2007, it was still at an early stage. But now, the cancer has spread. Surgery, radiation, chemotherapy—that would cost at least twenty thousand yuan. I mend clothes, one yuan to patch a hole or sew on a button. There was no way I could get that much money. Even with the surgery, the doctors said I might only get five years or so. We didn't have money. I didn't even have a place to borrow money. And even if I had been able to borrow enough money to extend my life a little bit, it would take my family generations to pay it off. I'm a Chinese and I was born in a poor area. What can I do?

*Liao:* Your hometown served as a base for the Communists in the early revolution era. Chairman Mao mentioned the contributions of your hometown to the revolution in several of his articles.

*Li:* You are right. In the early days, folks in my hometown joined Mao in his guerrilla warfare and supported the Communist troops in the hardest of times. When the revolution succeeded, people were supposed to become masters of the nation, but their lives were even worse than before.

You see, we had no water. We dug wells, as deep as two people, but they were always dry. Water was like gold. Rainwater was free, but that didn't last long. It tasted like muddy soup with lots of bugs in it. If you filled up a scoop, you could see the bugs wriggling in the water. In the dry season, every puddle was precious. Unfortunately, we had a very long dry season. During that time, everyone drove a donkey-drawn cart with a big bucket on top. We would climb hills to get water from five or six kilometers away.

Things have changed quite a bit now. The government has initiated a few water projects to help alleviate the situation. But, you know, before I left my village at the age of thirty, I had only ever washed in pouring rain, stark naked in the courtyard, our annual cleansing. After my first daughter was born, the midwife cleaned my wife and the baby with only a small basin of water.

*Liao:* Didn't you worry about infection?

*Li:* We never considered infection as an illness. People with cancer couldn't afford treatment, not to mention an ordinary infection. It would heal itself. In my hometown, there was a high incidence of stomach or esophagus cancers. If I remember correctly, the only person who could afford treatment was a respected teacher who used to work in the city and had since retired. After he got cancer, he was hospitalized and had surgery. All of his medical bills were covered by the government. The surgery was a success. It was such big news, almost unheard of before. When he came back from the hospital, the village had a huge celebration planned for him. The retired teacher contributed six hundred yuan. Local opera groups put up a stage and performed for three days. People came from faraway to watch the operas.

*Liao:* What was the average lifespan for people there?

*Li:* About sixty or something. There were exceptions. My grandpa lived to be eighty, but he had no idea how he had managed to live that long. My father was the healthiest in my family. In the fields, he was like a big bull, working from morning to night without a break. He died at the age of fifty. Poisoning. Before he went to work in the field, he sprayed insecticide all over his body to kill fleas. It was a hot sunny day. Soon, he was sweaty all over. I think the insecticides seeped into his skin through the open pores. He began to have a stomachache first. Then, the pain became unbearable. He stumbled back home and lay down in bed. I remember he let out a couple of screams first and then passed out. Before the stars came out that night, his body twitched a couple of times and then he was gone.

People usually used DDT or "666" powder. The insecticide my father used was more potent; the itching fleabites drove him nuts, and he wanted quick relief. Without water, people never showered or washed their clothes or bedding. Perfect for fleas.

*Liao:* Did many people get killed by insecticides like your father?

*Li:* It was pretty rare. We started to mess around with insecticides when we were kids. We first had some burning sensations, and some of us had patches of purplish scars. Then the skin would flake off. In some serious cases, the skin would be red and irritated. You might experience some wooziness. You could get over it in three or four hours. Gradually, your body would become accustomed to the poison. Besides, in the summer, after we sprayed the insecticide, we normally waited for it to dry before leaving the house. My father was so impatient and dashed out into the hot sun when he was still wet.

*Liao:* What did you do before you came to Yunnan?

*Li:* In 1988 I saw a newspaper ad about a school for tailors in the provincial capital, Taiyuan. I left the village and traveled to Taiyuan, using up all my savings to pay for the tuition and living expenses. After graduation, I returned to the village. I was the "famous tailor" who had seen the bigger world. It was right before the Chinese New Year. Many families would show up at my door, bringing new fabrics and asking me to tailor some outfits for them. You can't imagine how nervous I was, a new graduate without any experience at all. I had to improvise.

But I survived. A few years later, my skills had improved somewhat, and my stuff became presentable. In 1994 an uncle on my mother's side came home for a visit. He lived in Chuxiong, Yunnan province. It was right after my divorce, and I was feeling miserable. This uncle of mine urged me to come to Chuxiong and even paid my train fare. Still, the journey took four days.

*Liao:* Like the Chinese saying goes: a tree will die if it is replanted, but a person will thrive when he moves.

*Li:* I can use water that flows freely out of a tub and shower as much as I want. Sometimes, I feel guilty for being too extravagant. One night, I had a dream that I was sitting inside a bathtub. Then my fellow villagers popped up around me, swearing and cursing: You bastard! How could you waste so much water that can feed generations of people here? Then they started to bite me. I woke up in a sweat.

*Liao:* So, did you continue with your tailor business here?

*Li:* Yes. Initially, I worked for a tailor on Foreigner Street. Eventually, I started my own shop. There were lots of foreigners and foreigner wannabes in the city. You could spot all sorts of exotic and weird outfits around. It was really quite cosmopolitan. But I was a hick from Shanxi, and there was no way I could compete with the other tailors, so I decided to specialize in mending clothes—hemming, fixing zippers, and patching holes, that sort of thing. It was small money but it all added up. Just like that, I thrived. I arrived here when I was thirty-one. In fifteen years, I saved up quite a bit of money and was able to send some home.

*Liao:* Who is taking care of your business now?

*Li:* I don't have to worry about my business anymore. I closed it down. I'm too weak to handle the sewing machine. I don't have a lot of days left.

*Liao:* Do you feel lost?

*Li:* No, I'm not lost. God will make plans for me.

*Liao:* When did you start to believe in God?

*Li:* I had heard about Christianity when I was a child. I don't know
whether it was from textbooks or from newspaper reports, but we
were told foreign imperialists enslaved the Chinese people with
Christianity, that it was a type of spiritual opium. We were atheists.
There were no Christians in my village. Some old folks would light
incense and worship Buddhist and Taoist gods at some temples
during holidays. I used to look down on them, even condemning
them for being superstitious. After I arrived in Yunnan, my mind
was opened. I saw people of all colors and countries. I started to
hang out with some of them. We have Protestants, Catholics,
Muslims, Bahá'í believers, all sorts of faiths here.

I was a victim of the Communist atheist ideology. I had
nothing to cling to spiritually. I had no idea where the end would
be. Each time things started to trouble me, I planned a way to
escape, either through smoking or drinking, or simply burying
it down inside. My eldest daughter suffered from a severe fever,
which turned out to be meningitis. We didn't get her treatment
right away. She ended up having epilepsy, and later on she
became deaf and mute. She died before she turned nine. At that
time, my heart was bleeding all the time, but I didn't know what
to do and where to seek help.

When I first found out that I had cancer, I had a very hard
time thinking it through. I would count my days with my fingers
and say to myself: "I hardly have any happiness in life. What is
the meaning in life?"

*Liao:* If you had twenty thousand yuan, you could have had
treatment. Things might have been different.

*Li:* If I had the surgery, it might have prolonged my life another five
years. But what's the point? It would be like waiting for death.
Cancer is a blunt knife, poking me and slowly cutting me to
pieces. The pain is unbearable; it was all I could do to endure it. I
didn't even have the strength to commit suicide.

*Liao:* What changed?

*Li:* There was a person, Brother Yang. He was born in Baoshan,
Yunnan, and lived near here. He used to pass my store all the
time. As we got to know each other, he would come in and chat
with me, asking me about my life and business. One day, I told
him about my cancer. He was very shocked. He sat down and
heard my story. He was really worried about me. He said, "It will
cost you lots of money to treat the cancer." I told him that I didn't
have money. All I could do was wait for death to take me. He
didn't agree. He said, "Don't give up too easily. Come to believe
in God. God will offer a cure."

I didn't take him seriously. He visited me many times and would
say things like: "Old Li, with your current condition, having faith
in God is your only way out. The hospital can't help you. Your
relatives are helpless. The government can't help you. For ordinary
people like us, especially poor people like us, we have to have some
spiritual support and have faith. You are on the verge of death, so
why are you hesitating? Give yourself over to God."

At that, tears welled up in my eyes. To tell you the truth, I was
a pathetic living ghost but had been quite snobbish, worrying
about being corrupted or getting bad luck from others. But God
reached out to me again and again through Brother Yang. So I
said loud and clear: "God, take me."

Brother Yang said a prayer of deliverance for me on the spot.
The hustle and bustle on the street remained the same. The sun

continued to shine on the city. The tiles stayed on the roof, and
the birds perched on them, chirping as they always do. Nature
continued its way. I was the one who changed.

I followed Brother Yang, clutching both hands in front of my
chest, tears streaming down like raindrops. I tell you, I wasn't
overcome with grief. I felt grateful. For the first time in my life, I
didn't think about myself or about human beings. I was thinking
about God, who is above us, above all living things, above the
highest mountain and above Erhai Lake. My parents gave birth
to me, but God gave me life. I didn't know that before. Cancer
helped enlighten me, giving wings to my heart, which had been
downtrodden in the mud, and made it fly and feel the bliss of
heaven.

*Liao:* I'm touched by your poetic description. Tell me more about
Brother Yang.

*Li:* He's a minister from a local house church. He believes that going
to church doesn't necessarily make one a believer of Jesus. But as
you know, the government doesn't recognize the legal existence
of house churches. During Easter in 2008, I was baptized at an
old church here, which has over one hundred years of history.
Many Christians in the region are like me. We do both, attending
services at the church as well as at individual homes.

*Liao:* Since you were converted, has your health improved?

*Li:* The illness has probably worsened. It's harder and harder for me
to take food. I can feel the tumor stuck in here. For every meal,
I have to rely on luck. I would have some water first and then
take the food bit by bit. If I'm lucky, the passageway would open
up a bit and some food could go down smoothly. Sometimes,
water can't even go down. When that happens, I have to go
hungry. But I feel more relaxed and in high spirits. When I first
started praying, I used to harbor selfish thoughts. I was hoping

for a miracle, as if God owed me that. As a result, I was always
distracted. I would think that God was probably helpless. God
wouldn't save me. In the past forty-some years, I had lived
in misery, nothing but total misery. It wasn't easy to change
completely. My minister instructed me to pray for friends and
relatives, and pray for those who are caught in the disasters that
are happening in the world every day, and pray for individuals
and nations that are deep into crimes of injustice, greed, and
murder and refuse to acknowledge their crimes. We should pray
to the Lord to forgive those individuals and nations and give
them another chance for redemption. I should pray for others
and, if I'm deeply committed, the Lord will help me without my
knowing it.

*Liao:* You mentioned suicide before; would you still try to do it if
you could?

*Li:* Now I think it's a sin. All lives are given by God. Only he has
the right to end them. I used to have all sorts of illnesses, and I
had surgeries. I lived in a village without water. I thought life was
unbearable and I wouldn't be able to survive, but I did. I think a
natural death will be much more bearable than going through a
surgery or living in a village without water. Death will be like a leaf
falling onto the ground. My soul will float into the arms of angels.

## Epilogue

Liao published this story on an overseas Chinese language website.
John Zhang, a pastor at the San Mateo, California–based Bay Area
Reformed Evangelical Church, was deeply moved by the patient's cour-
age and raised funds through his nonprofit organization, Humanitarian
China, to cover the surgery. Li Linshan was able to undertake surger-
ies. At this time, the patient is on the path of recovery.

*Chapter 7*

## THE FELLOWSHIP

Li Linshan, the cancer patient, wanted me to go with him to a Christian service so I might better understand what God had done for him. It was dusk on August 18, 2009, as I left the house I was staying at in Dali and made for a nearby intersection where Li said he would meet me. It was a pleasant evening, with a warm southerly breeze and the sky smeared pink with clouds. The streetlights came on. I could see shadows of human activity flickering in the windows of low-ceilinged houses. Li was waiting for me, and we headed toward a suburban village through the east side of Dali's old town.

I was becoming used to the messy alleyways that connected the city with its rural suburbs. A mismatched mixture of new buildings and old houses lined the way. Gigantic machines spewed out dust from a stone quarry. Trucks and tractors ran amok on the narrow roads, squeezing pedestrians into single file along the sidewalks. Li Linshan seemed oblivious to the noise and bustle around us, shuffling along with ease. He began humming a hymn, which lifted my mood. The setting sun cast rich layers of purple shadow. I thought for an instant we were inside a half-finished oil painting.

Li said we were going to Ganjia Village, near Erhai Lake, though the chaotic mixture of tall buildings and low houses along our route gave no indication of where one village ended and another began. I simply followed Li, who said the area used to be a cornfield, but had recently been converted into pig and chicken farms. That explained the permeating stink in the air. It was not until we walked past a family-run grocery store and turned into a courtyard that I realized we had reached our destination. On the stairs to the house, two shabbily dressed women greeted us. They shook our hands enthusiastically and ushered us into the house, which was already so crowded with people that I imagined being submerged in a pot of steamy hot soup bubbling with noise and laughter. It was a sparsely furnished room, maybe ten square meters, with an extremely low ceiling. A double bed, an old Chinese-style armoire, and a pile of cardboard boxes filled half the space; squeezed into the other half were eighteen or so people occupying a small sofa and scattered benches and chairs. People stood up to make room for us, handing us candies and fruits. I found a seat against the wall, next to a tiny coffee table with a pot of plastic violets and a vacuum flask. Li was engulfed with greetings as soon as he entered, and a woman ushered him to the sofa, which someone jokingly referred to as "the throne of our honored leader." After maybe ten minutes the chattering died down and Li was asked to lead the hymn singing. He chose "God exists here . . ."

Li stood before his audience, hymnbook open, took a deep breath, and began what sounded like a howling song, but as everyone joined in with a distinctive mixture of accents, the cringing dissonance that reached my ears gradually resolved itself into harmony, like blending water with milk.

I had heard some Western hymns in movies, where church choirs of men and women, boys and girls, sang beautifully with trained voices to the accompaniment of organ or piano. Certainly, I could understand why some would call it divine. But what I was humming along to were secular Chinese folk songs, easy to follow and easy to remember. Some tunes reminded me of those songs of the 1980s when the Chinese public had just started to embrace pop music. I presume the hymn was by Xiao Min, a young farm girl from the central province of Henan. Featured in a documentary called *The Cross: Jesus in China,* which I had seen recently, Xiao Min claimed to be inspired by God and, with no musical training, created and sang hymns while working in the field. She continued to write melodies and lyrics after she was imprisoned. In a matter of a few years, she composed more than 1,200 hymns, which spread all over China. At my friend Wang Yi's house in Chengdu a few months before, they also sang a hymn by Xiao Min: *With tears and laughter, with songs and silence, / We've gone through ups and downs, / We've walked through the darkest valley, / We've climbed upon the highest mountains. / Year after year, the gospel, the salvation, the happiness and the elevation, / Blessings all over China.*

During Li's hymn singing, I noticed two women and a man merge into the crowd, and one of the women slid in next to me. She was young and had beautiful long dark hair, like those models in shampoo commercials. Her fragrance unsettled me. She smiled and asked to share a hymnbook with me, gesturing to her open mouth, urging me to sing louder.

During a break between the hymns and the testimonials, I struck up a conversation with the young woman. She said her Christian name was Ruth and revealed she was a preacher and leader of this particular Christian fellowship. She declined to tell me her Chinese name.

Ruth was dressed like an urban fashionista. She told me she was a member of the Bai ethnic group, that she used to engage in ancestor worship, and bowed to a variety of deities and gods. She had owned a store in the old section of Dali and set up a minialtar for the Taoist god of fortune. She burned incense every day, hoping that her business could prosper. She was married but grew worried when, after several years, she was unable to conceive:

*Ruth:* I visited a Buddhist temple, seeking blessings from the Guanyin bodhisattva. But life still didn't work out the way I wanted. My husband left me. Our family was broken. I totally lost myself. I was in no mood to run the business in Dali. So I came back and moved in with my mother in Ganjia Village. She is a Christian. One day she dragged me to the church. I found myself surrounded by old men and women. It felt very strange to be thrown into that group of senior citizens. It was awkward and comical.

Soon after that, I took a bus to Xiaguan. During the trip, a rock bounced up from under the wheel and shot through the window. It struck my foot. I screamed with pain. But the other passengers just sat there, like robots. Not a flinch. The bus was as quiet as a pool of water. I was dumbfounded by what had happened. How could it be possible? Was someone trying to send me a signal?

When I returned from the trip, I was very distracted and couldn't get over the incident. I went to find my mother, but she wasn't in her room. On a table, I saw a copy of the Bible, which had never held any interest for me, but I picked it up and flipped it open. The passage I read was Isaiah 54:1: "Sing, O barren woman, you who never bore a child; burst into song, shout for joy, you who were never in labor; because more are the children of the desolate woman than of her who has a husband."

I was stunned. How could the Lord know that I was barren? Was he encouraging me to keep trying? I was deeply moved. The following Sunday, I went to the church and said my commitment prayer. I felt like I was reborn. I had a new name, from the Bible book of Ruth. She was a brave woman who took on the responsibility of supporting her mother-in-law after her husband died. She gleaned the fields for fallen grain and picked up all sorts of jobs. Eventually, she gained God's blessings, married another man, and bore a son.

Soon all my friends began calling me Ruth. I volunteered to work at a school in a poor region deep inside the mountains. The school was sponsored by the church, and I was given three hundred yuan a month to cover food and basic expenses. Living conditions were really harsh. For a while, I wavered in my faith. One morning I woke up feeling awful and depressed. So I covered myself with my quilt and started praying. I asked the Lord to direct me to the right path. I prayed for about ten minutes before I heard someone mumbling something. There was a little girl in the bed next to me, and she seemed to be talking in her sleep: "Take it easy, Ruth. You will be fine." I woke her up and asked what she was saying. She was still half asleep and didn't understand my question. I gently raised my voice and said, "You just said something to me. Try to remember it." The girl sat up, and after a while she remembered her dream. "You were crying. Angels were patting your head with their wings and telling you to take it easy," she said.

Ruth's story was interrupted when a woman sitting next to us signaled for us to hush. Another round of hymn singing was about to begin, and then some of the members gathered that evening would talk about their experiences, an opportunity to pour their hearts out to their Father in heaven. Village women, many of whom were semiliterate, had long been deprived of the right to speak and did not so much "tell" their stories as perform them, articulating their ideas with eloquence, as if each had been a professional trained actress. Their stories were told with vivid anecdotes. The variation of tone and occasional outbursts of tears enhanced the effect, carrying their performances to a high emotional level. They were true storytellers. I was a meager scribbler compared with their gift.

Each time a story ended, the audience would respond with "Amen."

The fellowship meeting lasted about ninety minutes—an incomparable piece of theater quite unlike anything that might have been staged or contrived. Then came the "curtain call" and everyone stood: "In the name of Jesus Christ, Amen." There followed a brief silence before the room began to return to a secular state with eddies of chatter and laughter rising steadily in volume. My mind lingered on the scene that had just ended, turning over in my mind sounds and images. I found my notebook and, taking advantage of the relaxed and open atmosphere to interview the "brethren," learned that the fellowship group was started by Ruth's family. Many of her relatives were core members. Growing up in a family with generations of farmers, Ruth was the first to leave the village. Her fifty-nine-year-old mother had been a believer for nine years, and Ruth had joined the church six years before; they were the "veteran" Christians in the village.

Two of Ruth's uncles and aunts on her mother's side had just converted. The elder uncle, in his fifties, worked as a truck driver at a county electric power station. He was baptized at the end of 2008. In the old days, he lived in constant fear because his truck moved in and out of deep valleys and dark tunnels where mudslides and tunnel collapses were frequent, but since his conversion he had found that prayer kept him calm in danger zones and banished his fear. He was thus more energetic.

The younger uncle was a farmer, quiet and shy. He looked a little over forty. He had only joined the church two months before. The conversion was prompted by a sudden illness. The younger uncle suffered a myriad of illnesses, including gallbladder inflammation caused by stones. The doctor recommended surgery, but that was not an option.

"We wouldn't be able to afford to pay the bill," he said, "even if we sold everything we had." Without other alternatives, Ruth's mother suggested that he turn to Jesus. She believed that faith would assuage her brother's mental anguish and worries and help heal his physical ailments. For the past two months, he had mixed prayer with an herbal medicine prescribed by a village doctor. His condition improved. Ruth's mother had yet to persuade her husband to join the church.

Ruth introduced me to a friend who had brought her daughter along. The woman, in her midthirties, was animated and articulate. It was hard to imagine that this young mother used to be tormented by depression and insomnia, suicidal thoughts, and dependency on medication. "I have gotten rid of my long-term dependency on medicine. I always bring my daughter to the fellowship gathering. I'm putting her under the care of our Immortal Father."

Having overheard our conversation, a young woman stepped over, but before she opened her mouth, tears streamed down her cheeks. She began crying uncontrollably, and people around us quietly wiped their own tears. The woman's husband had been diagnosed with gallbladder cancer. The family had sold everything in the house to pay for his surgery, but it couldn't save him. He had just passed away. When she calmed down, she apologized and said faith had given her the strength to move on. She pulled a young girl toward us and continued, "My daughter is a fourth-grader. She and I read the Bible together. When she prays, she does a much better job than I do. If her father hears her in heaven, I'm sure he will be so proud."

Most women in the fellowship were middle-aged. One gray-haired grandma caught my attention; I thought she might have been a seasoned Christian. Instead, she was a relative newcomer, having joined just three months earlier. She grew up fasting and chanting Buddhist mantras. She worshipped indigenous gods but also attended Christian churches when she was young. Like most Bai people, she was carefree with her worshipping and was prepared to accept anything she felt was useful to her. One day on her way home from the fields, she suffered a stroke and collapsed by the side of the road. Ruth happened upon her and took her to a hospital. Timely treatment saved her life. After the woman recovered, Ruth started preaching the gospel to her. Since the woman was partially deaf, Ruth would raise her voice and shout in her ear. Now, each time the woman's heart becomes constricted, she clutches her chest and prays and immediately feels better.

I spent the remaining few minutes with a couple from my native province of Sichuan. We talked in the Sichuan dialect. They both grew up in Anyue County and moved to Dali more than eighteen years earlier. They had been in the marble and granite business. The wife did most of the talking, while the husband kept nodding. When she and her husband first arrived in Dali, they held temporary jobs and worked long hours. When they had saved enough money, they opened their own store selling marble slabs. In their spare time, the wife said, she would play mahjong:

*Wife:* Ten years later, I became a mahjong addict and would play whenever I found a spare moment. This shouldn't surprise you. As you know, Sichuan is probably ranked as the number one mahjong province. Everyone knows how to shuffle mahjong tiles. Mahjong involves gambling. Ordinary folks bet ten or twenty fen for fun. In some circles, the bets are much higher. At the beginning, I didn't see my addiction as a serious problem. I thought I could kick my habit very easily. I was wrong. I picked up mahjong easily but couldn't put it down. When I was craving a round of mahjong, it didn't matter what else I was doing. Nothing would stop me. When I had my first child, I would nurse him with one hand and move the tiles with the other. I lost money big time. Each time I lost, I would go pray at a temple, burning incense, hoping merciful Buddha would grant me some luck so

I could win the next time. If I won, I would donate part of the proceeds to the temple.

I wasn't well educated, but I was pious. I set up an altar in my home and worshipped the god of fortune and goddess of compassion every day. Even so, my lot never changed. I continued to lose big. My husband tried to talk me out of playing it, but I wouldn't listen. He became frustrated. Out of anger, he picked up the habit himself and fell into a bottomless pit. With two gamblers in the house, we fell deeply in debt. Sometimes we didn't even have money to buy food. Even so, we couldn't escape our addictions. We both ended up getting sick. Many people thought we were hooked on heroin. In truth, it was a type of heroin.

Luckily, we ran into Ruth, who generously helped us when we had no place to go. I heard a sermon one Friday evening. On the following Sunday, I participated in this fellowship group and was on my knees to make my commitment prayer. I changed my name to Yuc Lang—Bright Moon—to mark my rebirth that moonlit evening. When I went home that night, I bundled up the statues on my altar and my mahjong tiles and tossed them into a river. I cleaned the house, inside and out, and was soaked in sweat. It felt good. I had suffered insomnia for four years, but as soon as I fell into bed, I was asleep and slept through to the next morning. When I awoke, I opened the windows and felt the fresh breeze. That was 2005. I have played mahjong just once since then. I couldn't concentrate. I knew I had sinned. When I got home, I was on my knees, praying, and my husband saw me and asked, "What is this for? Is it worth it?" That night, I dreamed about a cross, shining so brightly it hurt my eyes.

I have not played since then. Our family situation has changed for the better. I no longer have insomnia. I'm quite healthy. My husband has even given up smoking. I don't have to beg the Lord for anything. He knows everything. Each time I make some progress, he would reward me with his blessing. I'm going to follow the path of the Lord and seek redemption until I die.

By eleven o'clock, the Christian brothers and sisters were making their farewells. Since I was the only nonbeliever in the group, people took turns urging me to remove my worries and submit myself to God. The simplicity and sincerity in their offerings touched me. They believed that faith was a valuable gift, and they wanted to share this spiritual awakening with a guest. At the crossroad, I parted with my friend Li Linshan, who leaned on the shoulder of his wife and walked home, step by step. I watched as he shuffled down the street. I knew the cancer was eating him away, but he made steady progress toward the light of his home.

*Part II*

# THE YI AND MIAO VILLAGES

*Chapter 8*

## THE DOCTOR

Darkness in the countryside is truly dark, black-ink dark, when the clouds are out and the moon so new it has yet to be born. I had not seen darkness like it for years. With the chill wind whistling, I felt alone, though I knew my traveling companion was just an arm's length away. Dr. Sun (I will only use his family name because he wishes to avoid undue attention from the authorities) was taking me, on this dark night, to Fakuai Village in the mountains of Tianxin County in Yunnan province. "Fakuai," I learned, was slang in the local Yi language for "waist of the mountain," which was indeed where the village was located, though Dr. Sun was more precise when he explained we were going into the mountain's "belly button."

Dr. Sun, a missionary doctor I had met in 2004, agreed to introduce me to some Christian leaders in the ethnic Yi and Miao villages, where he visited three or four times a year. We had set out early enough, I thought, on December 9, 2005, but it was late in the day when our driver reached the end of the asphalt highway and his van began to shudder as its tires rumbled along a "hard candy" road, made from a mixture of mud and small stones. The driver, teeth now clattering, made no effort to slow down, and the van hurtled forward. Dr. Sun shrugged his shoulders—such was the violent shuddering of the van it was hard to tell—and grinned, "You just get used to it."

Dr. Sun was clearly well known in these parts; he was greeted like a lost brother as we entered the courtyard house of one of his assistants at about nine o'clock, the group sitting around the fire jumping at once to their feet and rushing to surround him. The owner of the house helped unload the bags of donated clothing we had brought with us. It was around midnight by the time the clothing had been distributed, the villagers had left, and we were left to soak our feet in basins of hot water set before the fire. Neither of us was sleepy, so we talked:

*Liao Yiwu:* It seems so surreal, sitting here with you, in this remote mountain village. It's so quiet and beautiful. When we first met, you told me you were born in the city of Nanjing. How did you end up in Yunnan province?

*Dr. Sun:* Both my grandparents and parents were herbal doctors. They used to run one of the oldest and most reputable hospitals in town and made quite a lot of money. They purchased lots of farmland as investments. When the Communists came, the world was turned upside down. My family became the target of persecution—members of the evil exploiting class. Their hospital was confiscated; so was their farmland. But they were well known for their medical skills, so they were considered valuable for local senior Communist officials. As a result, they escaped execution. It was hard being born into a family with such a murky political background. I was constantly taunted in school and banned from participating in many school activities.

In 1975, when I was in junior high school, I signed up as a volunteer and came to Xishuangbanna at the southern tip of Yunnan, about as far south as you can go. I joined a state farm. I was the youngest worker but lied about my age. I wanted to get out of Nanjing, get away from my family, to disappear.

You know, Xishuangbanna has many different ethnic groups.

The Dai people form the largest group; then there are the Hani, the Lagu, Bulang, Yao, Yi, Wa, and the Bai. It is easy to disappear here. I was assigned to Jinghong Commune, which was close to the border with Myanmar and Thailand and consisted of many Dai villages.

Living so far from the city, I thought I could get away from Mao's political campaigns. I was wrong. It was the same everywhere, but about ten years behind the cities. While major cities had shifted their focus of political attack from former landlords to intellectuals and government officials, the leaders in my commune were still holding public condemnation meetings against the landlords. The day I arrived, I met a young fellow, a Dai. He seemed nice. He even climbed trees like a monkey to get fruit for us urbanites. We didn't know he was the son of a rich landowner until the local militia beat him up. He was beaten up a lot.

My disappointment with society and my doubts about Communism started there, I think. The older I got, the more reactionary I became. I came to realize that all those political slogans—"People are masters of the country," "The Party is always great, glorious, and correct"—were utter nonsense.

One day in 1976, as I was harvesting bananas, the farm's loudspeakers began blaring mourning music, and the announcer's deep voice said our great leader, Chairman Mao, had passed away. I kind of laughed and thought how we used to chant "long live, long live" every day, and then he dropped dead, just like everyone else. What great news! Of course, I didn't share these feelings with any of the others.

Later, I was assigned to work at the farm's clinic. In 1977, when China resumed the university entrance exam system, I passed all the tests and was enrolled in Beijing Medical

University. Five years later, after I obtained my MD, I got a
job at a hospital affiliated with the Suzhou Medical College,
close to Shanghai. I became a surgeon, working in the ER
department. I handled all sorts of terrible cases—ruptured livers,
disembowelments, severe head injuries, severed limbs. That was
where I honed my surgical skills. By 1988 I was promoted to be
an administrator, and in 1995 I became the deputy dean of the
medical school.

*Liao:* You were young and had a bright future.

*Sun:* A critical skill of an ER surgeon is to diagnose fast and
accurately, and then act. You can't play games. But as an
administrator, none of the skills I had acquired applied. They
played by a different set of rules. In my leadership position,
I initiated some reform measures. The school assigned me a
Santana car, but I asked the authorities to sell it and spend the
money on the hospital. I rode my bike to work every day. I
abolished the traditional big staff banquets during holidays and
banned the use of public money for eating and drinking. I also
tightened up on reimbursing expenses. All of those measures
hurt the interests of other leaders; they hated my guts and
conspired against me. It was very frustrating and depressing. In
early 1990 our college invited some foreign teachers and students
to teach and study there. It was through them that I got hold of
a Bible. I was examining my life at that time. I felt extremely
frustrated with my work as a deputy dean. The Bible taught me
to be in awe of God and to love, two important qualities that the
Chinese people lacked. Too many Chinese will do anything for
trivial material gains and have no regard for morality, ethics, or
the law. How do we change that? Can we rely on the Communist
Party? Can we rely on government rules and regulations?
Apparently not.

In September 1990 I participated in a prayer session at a foreign student's dorm. It was the first time I ever prayed. I saw several Chinese students there. I began to attend Sunday Mass at private homes and gradually formed the habit of praying before bed every night, reflecting on what I had done that day and how I might do better. In the winter of 1991 I went on vacation to Xishuangbanna. It happened to be Christmas. While I was attending a Christmas celebration at a Christian's home, my heart was touched in a way it had never been touched before. With the help of a missionary from Germany, I was baptized.

*Liao:* Could you be both a Christian and a government official?

*Sun:* I felt I had to make a choice, but that choice was largely made for me. One of the students at my first private prayer session ratted on me. In 1997, my boss came to me with an application form for membership in the Communist Party. He told me that by joining the Party, I would be able to dispel the "rumors" about my association with the Christian movement, that I had been in the system for many years and had established myself in the medical field, and that it was a minor concession that would open a lot of doors for me.

I told him I could not fill out the application form. I said, "What you heard are not rumors. It is true." My boss was shocked and pretended not to have heard what I said. "I believe in Jesus Christ," I said. "I have already made my choice, and this is the only choice."

He was tremendously upset. "You are a Communist official. You enjoy the salary and the benefits of a Communist official, yet you believe in Jesus Christ. What can you do with Jesus? Can he provide you with food and clothing?"

I looked him in the eye and said, quite deliberately: "I am quitting now. I need to save my soul."

The hospital relieved me of all my duties, and I had to leave the medical school. Soon after, Jinghong Hospital in Xishuangbanna hired me, but it didn't work out. I tried the Shenzhen Special Economic Zone and eventually landed in Thailand where I traveled to the beautiful northern city of Chiang Mai. I was recruited as a volunteer by a hospital sponsored by an international humanitarian organization and went to a poor mountain region in Myanmar, which was ravaged by war, epidemic diseases, and poverty. There were poppy plants everywhere and gun-toting guerrillas, who looked more like bandits. I heard shooting sometimes. The "hospital" was several sheds with thatched roofs in the middle of a forest, but it had some highly skilled doctors, many of them from the West, who came on rotation.

*Liao:* How did you communicate with patients and fellow medical staff?

*Sun:* Many of the patients spoke Chinese. I also knew some Dai and English. The conditions there were rough, but we had amazingly amicable working relations. We all took our jobs very seriously, and it was not unusual to work for days without a break. I learned a lot working there.

I returned to China in 1999. I had confidence, but not much else. My nephew helped get me a job as an adjunct professor in the medical school of the University of Yunnan.

*Liao:* With your experience, why not a big government-run hospital?

*Sun:* I'm a Christian. I found it impossible.

*Liao:* How could faith be an obstacle to your career?

*Sun:* It's not that. I couldn't work there out of conscience. Say a patient, tortured by illness, sits in front of you, staring at you, hoping you can find a cure for him. What kind of medicine should you prescribe? Many meds do the same thing, but their prices can vary sharply. I would prescribe the cheapest and most effective. But if I continued to do that, the pharmacy and the hospital would be upset because I have undermined their profits, disrupting the cozy deal between pharmaceutical companies and hospitals. When you break hidden rules and harm the collective interests of hospitals and doctors, you find yourself very alienated.

*Liao:* There is a saying in China now: "Doctors are like robbers, corrupt and unconscionable."

*Sun:* You are right. Doctors should be able to diagnose many types of illness with ease and treat them with the right kind of medicine. It should be easy, like pushing a stranded boat back into the flowing water. The reward is in helping the patient. But the reality is quite different in China. It now costs hundreds of yuan to see a doctor for even a minor ailment. Instead of a course of antibiotics or traditional herbs that costs ten or twenty yuan, and that includes a decent profit, hospitals want doctors to charge ten times that. It's greed. As a Christian, I have to tell my patients the truth. I cannot lie to get more money out of them.

*Liao:* So you were forced to become an "itinerant doctor."

*Sun:* Nobody forced me to do anything. One day I bumped into a former student of mine at the church. At first, I didn't recognize him; I taught so many students at the University of Yunnan. He told me he had grown up in the rural areas of Jiaoxi in Luquan County, which is deeper in the mountains, along the Jinsha River. His village is remote, but its people welcome outsiders. All the villages had converted to Christianity. My student told me that a woman in his village was dying of an unknown illness. He asked if I was interested in taking a trip there. I was noncommittal, but he showed up at my door the next day, so I went with him. It

took us the whole day to get there by long-distance bus. It was
the wife of a local minister who was ill. I examined her. She had
breast cancer; the tumor was as big as an egg. She needed surgery
right away. The minister explained that he had taken his wife
to various hospitals in the provincial capital city of Kunming,
but they wanted eight thousand yuan to do the operation. He
had gone to relatives and fellow villagers, but all he could raise
was two thousand yuan. I told the minister that I would do it for
free, that I had done far more complicated surgery than what
was required here, and he needed to trust me. He looked at me
in disbelief, as did the villagers gathering around us. I'm not sure
which of my assertions they had the most trouble believing.

I wanted to take the woman back with me to Kunming so I
could use a proper operating room, but she didn't want to leave
her home. That night, I knelt and prayed, and as I was praying,
an old American TV show popped into my mind—a team of
cheerful doctors doing surgery while cracking jokes, a mobile
army hospital, tents in an open field, the war in Korea.

*Liao:* You must be talking about the TV show *M*A*S*H*. I've seen a
couple of episodes.

*Sun:* Yes. I felt inspired. The next day, I bought some basic surgical
instruments to supplement the ones I carried with me, and we did
the operation in her bedroom. Her bed was a wooden plank; no
table necessary. All we had to do was clean up the room a bit and
we could do it there.

*Liao:* Did anyone assist you?

*Sun:* Yes, another minister in the village. He was in his sixties, a
grandpa figure. The room was very dark; even after we opened
all the windows, it was still pretty bad. I tied four flashlights
together and had the grandpa hold them as operating lights. That
grandpa was strong and in great health. He stood there for hours

without moving, holding the light steady. I removed the tumor, which took quite a while, but I didn't feel tired at all. It was a sweet feeling to be there with the poor villagers and to do God's work, though I never thought I'd ever have to perform surgery in quite those conditions.

After the surgery, news spread faster than wind, and I was inundated by villagers seeking help. I ended up staying for more than a week, including an eight-hour trek on foot from Jiaoxi to Zhaji in Wuding County. There was no road. I climbed hills, crossed rivers. By the time we got there, my shoes were almost worn out. I was quite a hiker, but that trip was the longest and toughest I had ever done.

*Liao:* I know the area. Locals use donkeys to carry their goods, and the animals slip and fall into the ravines all the time.

*Sun:* After the climbing and walking, I slept soundly and did two surgeries, one related to chin cancer and the other skin cancer. Both went smoothly. I had found my path and mission.

Yiliang County in Shaotong region is one of the poorest in Yunnan. The mountaintops have been cut bare of trees and villages are scattered. People live in low thatched houses with doors like cave entrances requiring you to stoop to get in. In one village I visited, people relied on two wells to draw water, one for livestock and the other for humans. When drought hit the region, villagers had to carry water from a river at the foot of a mountain.

I traveled there on several medical missions. Sometimes we had no cleaning water, and I would go days without a shower or even washing my face. But I didn't mind it.

On one such trip, I encountered a Yi limping around on a rough crutch. One of his pant legs hung empty and one side of his face was twitching. When I inquired about his situation, he said he had lost part of his leg in a traffic accident. I asked if I could see and had him sit. I don't know what bastard did the amputation, but it looked horrible. Half of his right leg was gone and the bone of his thigh was poking out like a knife; the flesh around it had decayed and the stink was horrible. I told him: "I have to fix this, now, or you will die."

He looked at me, stunned at first, but he understood me and tears ran down his cheeks. I had to amputate the rest of his leg if I was to save his life. Soon, I found myself surrounded by a crowd. Nobody knew who I was, except that I had come from Kunming. But they were trusting and helped carry the man to his house and laid him flat on his bed. I took my instruments out from my bag, sterilized them and the infected area, injected anesthesia, and removed the gangrenous tissue.

I sorted out the blood vessels, and sewed them up, like a grandma sewing the soles of shoes, and started the amputation. The process is nothing mysterious. It's very much like carpentry. You need a saw, a file, a chisel, a hammer, and a planer. I carried with me a small saw with sharp teeth. The bone on the thigh of an adult is fairly tough; not as hard as iron, but harder than wood. It's not easy to cut a man's leg off. My arms became numb from the vibration of the saw, back and forth, back and forth. Sweat poured down my face. If we had been at a regular hospital, the nurses would have helped, but all I had was untrained villagers, who simply stood there clueless. I smoothed and rounded the cut bone with a hammer and a chisel and sewed up the healthy skin and flesh.

On another occasion, I had gone to the Red River Prefecture, where the famous Red River Cigarette Factory is located. I visited a leprosarium to operate on someone with appendicitis. None of the doctors in the area would treat him. One had some medicine delivered but wouldn't go there for a diagnosis.

Appendix removal is relatively minor surgery, and I thought nothing of stopping by to do the operation, though the patients in the wards there were surprised. "You certainly have guts to visit us here," they said. The patient was a middle-aged man; his hands and feet appeared deformed because of all the dead and dying skin. He was very calm, never complained about pain. A Catholic girl from Gansu province assisted me with the operation. It went smoothly. It was a straightforward procedure done under local anesthetic. After we stitched him up, the patient nodded his appreciation and slowly walked back to his ward.

Speaking of leprosy, as I was waiting for a bus on the side of a road near Shimenkan one day, I saw in the distance a thatched house half hidden among the trees on a hill. Thinking it might be the residence of a hermit or a scholar, I decided to pay a visit. The guide looked scared and stopped me: "That is the home of two leprosy patients." Driven by curiosity, I ignored the guide's warning and went. I saw an old couple dozing off in the sun. When I examined them, I saw that neither displayed any leprosy symptoms. They were quite healthy people.

The old man, Zhang Zhi-en, used to live in a village nearby. In the 1970s, while digging herbs in the mountains, he ran into a snake, which the locals called Ma snake. He killed it with a berry hoe. When he related the story to his fellow villagers, they spread rumors that he had leprosy. According to local folklore, people would contract leprosy if they encountered a Ma snake, the name of which sounded similar to leprosy. He was locked up in a local sanitarium for years. His ex-wife, who had also been accused of having leprosy, was burned to death when she was still alive, bedridden with another illness. The old woman I saw that day was his second wife. Their life was quite miserable. Nobody talked to them. Part of his house had collapsed, but he didn't have the means to fix it. I contacted the local church and donated two thousand yuan myself to the renovation project. We put tiles on the roof, and it looks really nice now. We even bought some pigs and chickens for him to raise. His life is much improved. He's now accepted by people in his church.

*Liao:* Tell me about the young fellow, Little Sun, from the village of Malutang.

*Sun:* He used to be a temporary worker at a shipyard in the city of Guangzhou, married, with children. Life looked quite good for him until he lost the use of his legs. He sought treatment all over the place. A well-known professor at the Zhongshan Medical University examined him, but just shook his head. As his paralysis progressed, his wife left him. His fellow workers sent him back to his native village, where his parents had to take care of everything for him, from eating to bathroom needs. It was all very tragic. Surgery wasn't the solution, nor was Western medicine, but it came to me that traditional acupuncture might be the answer. I didn't have any formal training in acupuncture, so I took lessons from a well-known Chinese herbal doctor, Mr. Liang. It was truly a fun and rewarding experience. Once Mr. Liang signed my certificate, I went to see Little Sun, and he agreed to try the treatment. After my first visit, he said his legs hurt, so he could feel them. We kept up the treatment. At the same time, I prescribed some herbs. Slowly, he was able to stand, and now he can walk without a cane. He is taking medical lessons from me and can take care of common ailments.

*Liao:* He's opened a barbershop in the township, where he also does dental work.

*Sun:* I introduced him to a visiting dentist from America. Little Sun received training from him. I'm told he's pretty good at it now.

*Liao:* I've met quite a few of your students.

*Sun:* In the past eight years, I have trained thirty or forty, and
we now have a rudimentary rural medical network. While it's
important to have professionally trained doctors available, it's
more urgent and realistic to have people on the ground who have
some basic medical knowledge. In the rural areas, when there is
an emergency, it takes time for a doctor to get there. Life is really
hard for villagers in these mountainous regions, which are hours
from the nearest township, and even there the hospitals are poorly
equipped and staffed. It's okay if you are well and healthy. But
once a villager gets hit with a sudden illness, he is in big trouble.
Many people die each year from what are really minor ailments
and injuries.

*Liao:* But setting up and running a rural medical network is a
government job.

*Sun:* The Communist Party is rotten; how can we rely on this
government? Some overseas charity organizations have been
very helpful, but their help is temporary. Mostly, we have to
rely on our own local resources. In 1999 I contacted a charity in
Singapore. They sent over three doctors, one from the United
States, one from Hong Kong, and one from Singapore. We visited
this area. That was when we met another man named Sun. He
lives in Dazhuji Village in Zehei County. He had some medical
background and was running a small clinic, but he was deep in
debt and his clinic was facing bankruptcy. The charity offered
financial help. But I think, more important, we gave him the
confidence that he badly needed. I said to him: "Foreign aid is
certainly good, but you can't rely on it. You have to figure out a
way to use local resources. The best way to do this is to tap into
Chinese herbs. They are readily available in the region." Over
the years, Mr. Sun has been able to help others and pay off his
debts. He is now doing fairly well.

*Liao:* I met two Chinese American doctors at your house in
Kunming. Have they been of help?

*Sun:* They traveled to the rural regions several times and were
willing to make some financial contributions. They have seen
what it is like in China's remote areas. I advised them to stay
away from government officials so their money can directly
benefit the rural villagers.

But I have to admit that our help is limited. Many times we
are helpless in the face of human suffering. In a remote village
in Jiaoxi, I met the village leader who has a large tumor on his
neck. Initially, it was a small one and some doctor tried to remove
it, but he didn't root it out. The tumor returned and grew bigger
and bigger. When I met him, the tumor had already spread to his
left shoulder and the back of his head. It was so heavy he couldn't
keep his balance while standing. It was cancer of the lymph nodes
and had advanced to the stage where an operation was no longer
possible. All I could do was sit with him. I read to him from the
Bible and said, "Your life in this world is finite, but to God it
is infinite." He nodded at me and smiled. I held his hands and
stayed with him quietly for an hour. He died the next day.

One time I was taken to the house of a fifty-year-old woman.
She was fighting for her breath and in a lot of pain. She was
bleeding internally, and it was too late for any treatment. I asked
for a basin of warm water and washed her face and combed her
hair. As a doctor, I could do nothing for her. But as a person, I
could give her back some dignity. I sat with her, held her hands.
Her breathing was heavy, painful. I felt very sad for her. So I
whispered: "Big sister, I know that you have suffered a lot in
this life. Don't be scared. Don't be afraid. It will be over. The
gate of heaven is wide open for you. Your sufferings will end
there." Tears ran down the sides of her face, her body twitched a

couple of times, and a few minutes later, she passed away. Things happened pretty fast.

Now, let me tell you an uplifting story. In the summer of 2001, I was traveling in the Jiaoxi region and stopped at a village. It was about three o'clock in the afternoon. After I had rested for an hour, a local official asked if I would see a man who was dying of a mysterious illness. It was a two-and-a-half-hour walk along muddy mountain paths. I slipped and fell several times. It was eight o'clock when we arrived. I remember the sun was setting behind the hills. There must have been about a hundred villagers surrounding the patient's dark thatched house. A red casket was outside the door, its cover wide open. It was quite spooky. The patient was coughing blood; there were bloodstains everywhere. He seemed to be on the verge of death. His family members told me that he had lung cancer and showed me his X rays. The patient was quite lucid. I gave him an injection to stop the bleeding and asked him for the history of his illness. After an examination, I was sure it was not cancer, but tuberculosis, still quite serious. I didn't have any TB meds with me. The next morning I set out with the patient's two daughters for Kunming, which we reached midafternoon, and sent them back with some medicine and instructions on correct dosage. When I called three days later, the casket was gone from his door and his condition was improving. A checkup three weeks later confirmed he was making a speedy recovery.

*Liao:* You wander around the rural areas, providing these services to people. How do you support yourself financially? Do you charge people for treatment?

*Sun:* In the first two years, a church organization in the United States provided some financial support so I could do my charity work. I developed a close friendship with a young woman at that organization. Later, her boss changed his mind and stopped the financial aid. But I put my trust in God. I don't have a lot of expenses. The only money I need is for bus or train fares. When I travel from village to village, I stay at the homes of local peasants who feed me a bowl of rice and beans.

*Liao:* But that's not really a long-term plan.

*Sun:* People are really kind. Some peasants insist on paying for treatment—ten or twenty yuan. Those requiring more complex treatment offer two hundred to three hundred yuan. I have some contacts willing to let me pay wholesale for meds, and the money the peasants give me covers those costs. In the past two years, some doctors abroad have learned about me and are interested in what I do. They contribute medicines, and the two Chinese American doctors have rented a place in Kunming to use when they are here; I look after their patients when they are in the United States.

*Liao:* I stayed at their office once.

*Sun:* The place can accommodate six people at a time. There are enough doctors in big cities. I think I'm going to spend the rest of my life here. It fits me perfectly.

Epilogue

In 2009 Dr. Sun caught the attention of Yunnan government officials, who accused him of harboring "ulterior motives" by treating the poor for free and subsequently banned his medical mission in Yunnan. Meanwhile, after Liao published Dr. Sun's story on an overseas Chinese website, he received an invitation from a Chinese church in the United States to talk about his work. He arrived in the United States in 2009 but has not been allowed to return to China. He now resides in California, trying to improve his English skills and seek missionary opportunities in Africa.

*Chapter 9*

# THE MARTYR

Above the Great West Door to Westminster Abbey in central London stand ten statues recognizing Christian martyrs of the twentieth century from around the globe. One of those statues is of Wang Zhiming, who lived and preached in Wuding County in China's Yunnan province and served the ethnic Miao. Arrested in 1969 for his religious work, he was executed in 1973. He was sixty-six years old. Wang Zhiming's story was well known within the Christian community in Yunnan, but outside the circle most Chinese have never heard of him. His family members, many of whom have continued his cause, rarely talk to the mainstream media.

I first heard of Wang Zhiming in December 2005, when I was traveling in Yunnan with Dr. Sun, who was an acquaintance of Wang Zhiming's son, a well-known Christian leader. I tracked him down in January 2007.

The church in Xiachangchong Village, Gaoqiao Township, is an impeccable white, with a pink roof, and reminded me of a magic castle against the backdrop of high mountains. Leading to it are raised muddy paths, along one of which a local villager led Dr. Sun and me. We followed him up and down hills and through gullies of bush and vine. Near the village entrance stood Wang Zisheng, the son of Wang Zhiming. He had been tipped off about our arrival and greeted us like long-lost brothers, shaking hands, patting shoulders.

Wang Zisheng, born in 1940, had just turned sixty-seven. He was short, sturdy, like a tree stump, with a big cotton hat. We followed another path that snaked around the village before reaching his courtyard house, a chaotic "farm" with pigs, dogs, and chickens all about and the pungent smell of their doings assailing my nose. When Wang Zisheng opened the door to let us into the house, a mother hen and a dozen chicks slipped between our feet and vanished inside.

The first interview, taking place inside the house, lasted four hours. After we bid him good-bye and walked out of his courtyard, Wang's wife caught up with us, tucking some oven-baked buckwheat cakes into our hands. I never felt so hungry and gobbled them up right away.

Six months later, as I was transcribing the interview, I noticed that half of Wang's stories had been accidentally erased from the tape. I examined the machine back and forth, banging my head against a wall. During the previous ten years, I had done more than two hundred interviews. That was my first accident.

Out of desperation, I phoned Dr. Sun, begging him to arrange a second interview. So on August 5, 2007, I traveled to Kunming and met up with Dr. Sun.

The mishap with Wang Zisheng's tape was only the beginning of a series of misfortunes. On the way to Kunming's bus terminal, I left my bag on the backseat of the taxi. The bag contained some of my most prized possessions—a flute that had followed me for many years, a camera, a new tape recorder, my notebook, and some of my favorite music CDs. Visiting the police station and phoning the taxi dispatcher produced nothing. I had to press on with my task. I reorganized myself, purchased a new tape recorder, and returned to the bus station only to find it jammed with people on their way to a nearby festival.

The whole world seemed to have risen up against me, and while Dr. Sun suggested we go another time, I stubbornly refused. We finally persuaded a truck driver to take us. As we sat in traffic jams due to a harrowing accident, I bowed my head and prayed like a Christian, asking God if he was testing my patience and confidence. Before dusk, as our truck was approaching the white church building with the pink roof outside Wang Zisheng's village, my heart was filled with gratitude.

Wang was tending crops in the field. He looked a little confused when he saw us. As we slowly walked to his house, the sun was disappearing behind the mountains. Then two rainbows suddenly emerged in the sky, forming a colorful cross. For a few minutes, I became distracted by the unique natural phenomenon.

The lightbulbs glowed weakly inside Wang's cavernous room, so we all sat on the porch outside. Amid the attacks of swarms of post-summer-rain mosquitoes, our second interview started. I checked and rechecked my tape recorder. It was working.

By nine o'clock, I finally completed my mission and felt an overwhelming sense of relief. Fortunately, erasing an interview from the tape could be made up with the help of devoted friends like Dr. Sun. But what if we, as a nation, collectively lose our memory of our past?

*Liao Yiwu:* Why is it that Christianity has become widely accepted in the Miao villages?

*Wang Zisheng:* Christianity was first introduced to the Miao villages around 1906 with the arrival of two Christian ministers, one from Australia—his Chinese name was Guo Xiufeng; one of my relatives who reads English says his name is Arthur G. Nicholls—the other, an Englishman. I only know his Chinese name: Shi Mingqing. They belonged to the China Inland Mission and came here from Kunming on donkeys. They had traveled for three or four days, and when they finally reached the Miao villages, the two caused quite a stir. The Miao people had never seen anyone with blond hair, green eyes, and a big crooked nose. Both ministers were very tall, much taller than the Miao. They attracted lots of attention.

Since ancient times, the Miao people have lived in the mountains—farming, hunting, raising silkworms. We were quite primitive, no better than those birds flying in the sky or animals running on the ground. Throughout history, the central government has tried to conquer the Miao tribes.

The Miao people worshipped all sorts of spirits and ghosts and held to many traditions and customs. Each time we planned an event, big or small, good or bad, we would first burn incense to worship and seek protection from various gods and deities. For weddings and funerals, we had to invite Taoist priests or a shaman to our homes, paying them to perform all sorts of rituals, such as playing gongs, dancing, and chanting to drive away any evil spirits. Families here were as poor as the rats living inside the field burrows, but they all had to put on extravagant shows. If a person passed away, his family would slaughter pigs and goats, inviting everyone in the village to a wake that would last a whole week. At the same time, the family had to provide food and drinks to every visitor. People couldn't bury their dead right away. They went through rituals to show other villages that they had fulfilled their filial obligations. They also worried that if they didn't, retribution would come to them later. As a result, a dead person often ended up lying in the casket for ten to twenty days before the burial. Oftentimes, the corpse began to stink and decay.

The year the foreign Christian ministers arrived, the region was experiencing a terrible disaster, the worst in years—a pandemic. Within a ten-mile radius, there wasn't a single family that was well-off. There were dilapidated houses everywhere.

After a heavy rainstorm, when people's houses collapsed, they didn't have money to do the repairs. Humans and animals lived in close quarters under the same roof. When you were poor, you didn't have the luxury to care about things like personal hygiene. As a consequence, bubonic plague and typhus swept through villages like the wind. People dropped dead soon after they were infected. There wasn't enough time to bury the dead. Sometimes, three or four bodies would be dumped in one hole. Even so, there were bodies everywhere.

The two foreigners on donkeys went to dangerous places from where others were running away. As long as someone was still breathing, the ministers would feed them medicines. For those who couldn't be saved, they would squat beside the dying villagers, bow their heads, and say a prayer for them.

The Christian ministers also helped people rebuild their houses and restore their lives. They taught locals to segregate the living quarters between animals and humans. They taught everyone how to protect their water sources and pay attention to personal hygiene. They also helped people see through the deceptive tricks of the local sorcerers. Many survivors abandoned their practices of spirit or ghost worshipping and became Christians. As people changed their old ways of living, the ministers began to teach them how to read the Bible and how to pray. In the end, they decided to make Sapushan the base for their missionary work. They built a church, the first in Yunnan province.

People found spiritual support in the church. Every Sunday, people of different ethnicities—the Miao, the Yi, and the Lisu— would come from all directions and gather inside the church to hear the gospel, to hear the Word of God. On weekdays, they prayed at home or together in their villages. Many parents brought their children, asking the foreign Christian ministers to

name them. I don't remember my grandfather's original name,
but it was changed to Wang Sashi by the Australian minister, Guo
Xiufeng. My grandfather's new name meant "abandon the secular
world to pursue the path of the Lord."

My father, Wang Zhiming, was born in 1907. That was the
second year after the foreign Christians arrived. Our family
lived in Bajiaojing Village then, in Dongcun Township in Fumin
County. He started attending a local school in 1921, when he was
fourteen years old. Three years later, my grandfather transferred
him to a school run by the church in Sapushan. He graduated
in 1926. He was nineteen. The church assigned him to teach in
schools and preach in Haoming and Lufeng counties. He returned
to Sapushan in 1935 and continued to teach and preach in nearby
villages. When the resistance war against Japan started two
years later, the two foreign pastors left to take up assignments
elsewhere. My father was chosen to be the preacher at the main
congregation in Sapushan. In 1944 he became president of the
Sapushan Christian Association.

*Liao:* So Sapushan was where Christianity in the Miao ethnic region
started and developed. How big was the parish?

*Wang:* It encompassed all the Miao churches in five counties:
Wuding, Luquan, Fumin, Lufeng, and Yuanmou. It was the
largest Miao parish in Yunnan. Since donkeys were the main
means of transportation, preaching the gospel meant days on the
road, climbing up and down the mountains. It was very tough.
But under the leadership of my father, the parish developed
fast. According to documents that I have obtained, before the
Communist takeover in 1949, about 5,500 Miao, Yi, and Lisu
people were converted and joined the church group in Sapushan.
In 1945 my father went to live in the provincial capital of
Kunming for three months. He compiled a collection of psalms in

the Miao language. That was probably the first Miao hymnal in China.

When the Communists came, all religious activities were banned. In 1951, when I was eleven, my father traveled to Kunming and was ordained as a minister by Chu Huai-an, who had come from Shanghai. At that time, all foreign missionaries had been kicked out of China. The Communist government condemned foreign religions as spiritual opium, tools of invasion to oppress the Chinese people.

*Liao:* The Land Reform Movement started in 1951. Was your family affected?

*Wang:* Ours was a poor village. There were no landlords or rich peasants to persecute. Three relatively well-off households were put in the middle-class category, but the rest belonged to the class of poor peasants, allies of the revolution. But while my family was categorized poor peasant, we were Christians and received different treatment. We couldn't share any of the "fruits of the revolution"—we were not given land, housing, or money.

*Liao:* Without an evil landlord as its target, how did your village conduct its "class struggle sessions"?

*Wang:* We would import landlords from other villages to use as targets. People would raise their hands to condemn the landlords, tell their bitter stories about how they had been exploited, and then parade the landlords around in the field. You know, there were a lot of beatings and tortures. The village here didn't miss a single activity the campaign required. My father took pity on those fallen landlords. He would often sigh in private and say, "I don't know what's happening! Those kindhearted people leased their lands to us. They didn't even charge us that much money. It was very generous of them to do that. But now they are getting all this brutal treatment."

The government sealed and confiscated the church property in Sapushan and ordered my father to return home and farm under the supervision of the revolutionary peasants. Since he was one of the few literate people in the region, they made him the village accountant. He obeyed because the Bible says you should submit your body to the rulers, but he never stopped his daily prayers.

Sometimes, Christians in other villages would gather at our house late at night. The tense political environment made everyone nervous. All prayer activities went underground. Then the local government assigned members of the local militia to monitor us and interrogate us. They forced my father to confess his close ties with ministers in foreign countries. My father's situation made it very hard for him to connect with other local Christians, but he persisted. In 1954 the local public security bureau arrested my father on charges of "refusing to mend his ways and continuing to engage in religious and spying activities." He was sent to a prison in Luquan County.

*Liao:* How long did he stay in prison?

*Wang:* Not very long. You see, my father's case was unique; he was a prestigious figure in the ethnic Miao region. Since he had always worked hard in the field and obeyed orders, the government leaders decided, after careful consideration, to condemn my father publicly but at the same time make him a positive role model for other reactionaries. It would be good propaganda for Mao's thought-reform movement. So they released him in a few months and even appointed him to the preparatory committee of the Political Consultative Conference in the Chuzhou Prefecture. In 1956, as a Christian minister, he was made deputy of a delegation, which consisted of representatives from various ethnic groups in the region.

His delegation traveled to Beijing to join in the National Day celebrations. Chairman Mao even met with my father.

The meeting with Chairman Mao caused quite a stir here. The *People's Daily* carried the news with a big picture. But the Communist Party never trusted my father, and my father didn't believe in the communist cause. Even though he had met Chairman Mao, he was the target of every political campaign. He wrote many confessions and was the subject of many public condemnation meetings. By 1964, during the "Four Cleanup" campaign, my father was finally removed from all of his public posts and was kicked out of the revolutionary ranks. Again he returned to the village to farm under supervision. I think he knew the final destination for someone like him in an atheist society. He was waiting for that moment. He was never afraid.

In 1966 the Cultural Revolution started. The revolutionary masses swarmed into our courtyard, ransacked our house, and beat everyone. They tied us together and paraded us from village to village. My father was forced to wear a big dunce cap with the words "Spy and Lackey of the Imperialists." At public condemnation meetings attended by over ten thousand people, we were the targets of angry fists. The spit was almost enough to drown us. No matter how much we suffered, father never stopped praying. It went on like that for three years, until the revolutionary rebels began fighting one another and no longer had time to bother us. The daily harassment, for the most part, ended. My father found some former Christians, and they would gather inside mountain caves at midnight for prayer sessions. They didn't have a copy of the Bible, but they believed it was in their hearts. The Miao people were poor, but they were simple and honest. The government forced them to shout "Long live Chairman Mao," but it could not break their faith in God. So the gospel started to spread again in the nearby villages. My father continued to baptize people. Soon, the authorities learned about my father's activities. At dawn on May 11, 1969, my father was arrested. He had been in the mountains the night before for some baptisms. Someone must have informed on him.

*Liao:* Were you there when he was taken away?

*Wang:* I lived on one side of the road, with my wife and children. My parents and my little brother lived on the other. I was woken up by gunshots, louder than a thunderstorm. It sounded as if the mountain had cracked open. I saw three trucks with dazzling headlights. A thick crowd of people surrounded my parents' house. The flashlights they carried looked like stars on a summer night. I heard another bang, not a gunshot but someone kicking the door open. I heard loud screams, sharper than a knife blade. The soldiers were yelling. My mother was screaming back at them.

I sent my four children back into the house and told them to stay there. My wife and I were unable to cross the road, which was blocked by soldiers, so we took a roundabout route. By the time we got there, the trucks had rumbled away; I could see their lights heading into the mountains.

My brother told me what happened. Two soldiers guarded the entrance to the courtyard while two others, carrying loaded rifles with fixed bayonets, kicked the courtyard door open, fired two shots, and charged inside. They warned that anyone resisting would be shot on the spot. Inside the house, they found my father in bed and yelled, "Get up! Come with us."

My father was very calm. Without saying a word, he put on his clothes, but before his feet touched the floor, the two soldiers rushed forward and grabbed and twisted his arms. He looked

in their eyes and said, "No need to do that. I will go with you."
He then raised both of his hands, asking the soldiers to put the
handcuffs on him. My mother screamed and wouldn't let my
father go. The soldier kicked her. She fell and passed out.

By the time I arrived, my father was gone. My mother had
been taken back inside the house, and my brother's family stood
around her. She had become incontinent, her pants soaked with
urine. When she regained consciousness a few moments later,
she kept asking for water, saying: "I'm thirsty, I'm thirsty." She
drank several bowls and said her chest hurt. The pain stayed with
her the rest of her life.

My father was held for four years in Wuding County. In
December 1973 they executed him.

He was never officially accused, but they listed five charges
against him: first, he was a lackey of the foreign imperialists
and an incorrigible spy, using spiritual opium to poison
people's minds; second, he was a counterrevolutionary; third,
he consistently boycotted the government's religious policy;
fourth, he was a member of a local landlord gang; fifth, he led
a large group of evil landlords and their followers to ambush
the Communist Red Army when they passed through Lufeng
County in the 1930s, killing seven Communist soldiers. Local
Miao did exchange fire with Mao's army in Lufeng County. Both
sides suffered casualties. The battleground was far from here. My
father had nothing to do with it.

*Liao:* Were you able to visit your father before he was killed?

*Wang:* We could visit the detention center but were not allowed to
see him. We could drop off clothes, but not food. They wouldn't
give us any information about his physical condition. We were
constantly taunted by the revolutionary soldiers and villagers:

"Your old man was a bad guy. He believed in God. Why don't you draw a clear line with him?" "God is not the savior. Chairman Mao and the Communist Party are the saviors of the people? Do you believe in God or in Chairman Mao and the Communist Party?"

Eventually, we received a notice from the local government saying he would be executed. Since he was labeled "an incorrigible counterrevolutionary," the rules said we would not be able to see him. But since our family belonged to the Miao minority group, the government had granted us a final meeting, for "revolutionary humanitarian reasons."

On December 28, 1973, the day before my father's execution, members of the local militia showed up at our door and informed us that we could visit him. A dozen of our family members gathered, and we went together. It took us several hours to reach the detention center. After passing through several checkpoints and layers of high walls, we finally saw our father. His hair had turned gray; he was thin, like a skeleton. Each time he moved, the shackles around his ankles clanked loudly. As he hobbled toward us, we all cried.

He was treated the same as a murderer. Seeing that our whole family was crying and sobbing, one guard howled at us: "Stop crying! Hurry up and talk to your father one by one. Time is limited." He made us speak Mandarin so he could understand what we were saying.

My mother nodded at my father and said, "You are the one who used to do all the talking. We listen to you first."

My father smiled. He understood what my mother meant. "I haven't been able to reform my thinking," my father said in his usual tone of a Christian minister. "Since I cannot be changed, I am responsible for, and deserve, what I receive. But for all of you, don't follow me. Listen to what 'the above' tells you."

*Liao:* In secular terms, the word "above" means the government, but I assume that your father meant "God."

*Wang:* Exactly. Christians knew what he meant right away. Then he said, "You should engage in physical labor, making sure to have food to eat and clothes to wear. You should pay attention to personal hygiene and stay healthy. Don't get sick."

Our father's words warmed our hearts. He used to tell us that those were the words of his own father and the foreign missionaries. I stepped up to him and sobbed: "Dad, we will listen to what 'the above' tells us, but we have many children at home who need you. If you can't be reformed and come back home, what will the children do?" What I really meant was that he was a reverend and a leader of the church. His flock wanted its shepherd.

Then, my mother brought out six eggs and presented them to Father. My father reached out his bleeding hands, touched Mother on her head, her chest, and her shoulders, and then he separated the eggs, keeping three and giving back three.

*Liao:* The Trinity?

*Wang:* We understood the symbolism. At that point, a prison officer came in and announced, "Wang Zhiming has been sentenced to death. The execution will be carried out tomorrow after a public trial. The criminal's body shall be handled by the government. Family members don't need to get involved."

We begged the guard to explain why we could not take his body. He said that in response to the overwhelming requests from the revolutionary masses, the government had decided to blow up his body with explosives. We were shocked. We kept begging.

We promised not to erect a tombstone or put up any prominent signs that could bring people to pay tribute. The guard refused. "Throughout history, you Miao people are well known for being superstitious. Who knows what will happen if we allow your family to give him a proper burial!"

After Father was taken away, we refused to leave, demanding the right to collect his body. The prison officer became mad and summoned the local militia to drive us out. We did not resist them. It was already dark when we got home, and several dozen villagers were waiting for us there. They cried after hearing that my father's body would be blown up into pieces. We stayed home and prayed for God's help.

Early the next morning, a village official came and told us to borrow a horse-drawn cart. He said we could go to Father's public trial, which would be attended by ten thousand people. Afterward, we could, in his words, "drag home the body of the counterrevolutionary."

God must have heard our prayers, we said to ourselves. On the road, we quietly sang hymns together. The meeting site was packed with people shouting slogans and waving red flags. Two other criminals were also there on trial, but they wouldn't get the death penalty. They were dragged there to receive "education."

As soon as we arrived, several armed soldiers walked over and aimed their guns at us: "Don't move. Squat down with your hands clutching your heads." So we did, our backs toward the stage, but during the meeting, when the soldiers were distracted, we would quickly turn around to take a quick glance between people's heads at what was going on with our father. There were two rows of seats on the stage. All the county leaders were sitting there. My father, with his hands and legs tied with ropes, stood in the middle of the stage, the two other criminals on either side.

There was blood at the corner of his mouth. We learned later that a guard had used his bayonet to slash his tongue so he wouldn't be able to shout or preach. Some former church members and leaders went up on the stage and denounced my father's crimes. After that was over, a leader grabbed the microphone and announced, "Wang Zhiming has been sentenced to death; the execution will be carried out immediately." Soldiers raised Father into the air so everyone could see him. The crowd roared. They raised their fists high and shouted, but all I could hear were the words "Down with . . . ," "Smash . . . ," and "Long live Chairman Mao." There was a popular saying at that time: "When the revolutionary masses rejoice, counterrevolutionaries collapse."

The soldiers put a wooden sign on his back—a "death sign," it was called. It was half his height and listed the five crimes my father was said to have committed. His name was also there, with a big red *X* over its characters. The soldiers carried him to a truck and pushed him in with the other prisoners, bending his head low. Two cars led the way. My father's truck was in the middle. Another truck with fully armed soldiers followed. A machine gun was perched on the roof of the last vehicle. I was told they paraded my father around the streets for half an hour before taking him to an old airport where he was shot.

*Liao:* Where were you?

*Wang:* We were still at the meeting place, guns pointing at us. When most of the spectators had left, the soldiers tied all of us together with a long rope and led us to the detention center and a room where all of my father's belongings were on the floor. A public security officer said, "That's the garbage left by the counterrevolutionary. Take it home."

*Liao:* Weren't you supposed to collect your father's body?

*Wang:* Friends in the village did that for us. They had borrowed a cart, and when they reached the old airport, my father's body was surrounded by several hundred gawkers, like black crows. A soldier was guarding the body. Once he made sure the villagers were who they said they were, he let them take my father. We met up with them at the detention center. I wiped my father's face with a wet cloth. My sister covered his body with a quilt. It was one o'clock in the afternoon. It was sunny and the sky was blue. The road was empty by the time we left, the cart moving slowly, us on each side walking with it. I remember there were birds, flying and chirping, and it felt like Father was still alive all around us.

Some Miao people stopped our cart and said their good-byes to my father. Some were old, some young, some we knew, some were strangers. A little girl climbed onto the cart, opened the quilt, and touched my father's body, from head to toe. We smiled at her innocent gesture and for a moment forgot our grief.

By the time we reached the village, the sun had already set. We took my father's body inside the house. His face looked peaceful, as if he were just taking a nap. Village officials and members of the militia guarded the house to keep out visitors wanting to pay tribute, but after midnight, when the guards went home to sleep, fellow Christians quietly knocked and came in to pray with us.

*Liao:* How many people came that night?

*Wang:* Between seventy and eighty. They came quietly along the hilly paths, without flashlights for fear of being discovered. They were as quiet as sleepwalkers. By two in the morning, the last had finished their prayers and left. Our father's body was cold and stiff. He had left too.

At dawn, I went up the hill with my two brothers and my brother-in-law and spent about two hours there digging a grave.

After breakfast, we carried the coffin up the hill and placed it inside the hole. Then we went back to fetch our father's body.

*Liao:* Why did you separate the body from the coffin? Was that a Miao custom?

*Wang:* No, no. We had no choice. We didn't have enough strength to carry the coffin with Father's body inside. A truck with soldiers had arrived, apparently to prevent a possible riot among the Miao people. Soldiers with loaded guns were scattered around the village. Only family members were allowed to approach my father's grave. We had thought of having a brief funeral, but with the soldiers there, the villagers could only watch from about a hundred meters away. They were anxious to pitch in but couldn't do anything. It normally took eight people to carry a coffin, but there were only four men in my family. We tried several times but couldn't lift it. In the end, we had to separate the body from the coffin. The soldiers didn't leave until we had finished filling in the grave and returned home.

*Liao:* Many things changed in 1974. Chairman Mao and Premier Zhou Enlai were sick and approaching the end of their lives. The Cultural Revolution was winding down.

*Wang:* Yes, we could feel things change. Political control became somewhat relaxed; prayer and other religious activities resumed in our village. The local government found out and gathered all the Miao people for a meeting. One leader lectured us: "It's been only a few months since that counterrevolutionary was executed. You are not learning any lessons. Instead, you are meeting secretly to conduct religious activities. Your disregard for the Communist Party will be punished. Who is your leader? Step out!"

I was the first to step forward. In 1976 I was officially arrested and thrown in the same jail as my father. The public security officers said I was more incorrigible than my father. If my father's crimes were committed unintentionally because he had been brainwashed in the pre-Communist days, mine were premeditated. For the first four months, I was in solitary confinement, a small dark room with a concrete floor. The room had a porcelain bowl and a container for urine. I conducted all my activities—eating, drinking, peeing, and shitting—in that tiny space. I was in darkness all the time. A person cannot stay in darkness. A plant will die without sunlight. Animals go crazy after two weeks.

*Liao:* But a person can keep his sanity because he can think.

*Wang:* I had God in my heart. He kept me sane. During the Cultural Revolution, seven members of my family were persecuted; my father was executed; my second brother, Wang Zihua, who was dean of the People's Hospital in the Nujiang Lisu Ethnic Autonomous Prefecture, became a target of public condemnation. Wang Zihua couldn't take the beatings and the endless public denunciation. He jumped into the Nu River, committing suicide. My elder brother, Wang Zirong, followed the same path as I. We were arrested at the same time, both sentenced to eight years, and were released at the same time. I was sent to a labor camp in Yao-an County while my brother stayed in Luquan County. My mother's two sisters and one of my father's sisters were also arrested. They were sentenced to five and three years respectively for organizing and attending secret religious gatherings.

In 1979 China relaxed its control over religion and we were all released ahead of schedule after serving three years. In early 1980 the winds seemed to have changed in our favor. The government sent word that I was chosen to be a representative to the Wuding County People's Congress, a local legislative body. I couldn't refuse the appointment. I dug out my "sentence reduction

certificate" and showed it to the head of the local People's
Congress. I pointed out the words printed on the document:
"The criminal has confessed his crimes and is granted early
release on good behavior." I said, "How can a former criminal be
eligible for the position of a legislator?" The official went red in
the face and said, "They did a sloppy job. I'll look into this." A
couple of days later, I was issued a new document, which said I
was cleared of all charges. My father's name was also cleared after
they officially reversed the verdict. We were then able to build a
tomb for him.

*Liao:* I believe it is the only monument known to commemorate a
Christian killed in the Cultural Revolution.

*Wang:* In 1996 the church here held a big memorial service for
my father, the largest in history; the choir alone numbered two
thousand.

*Liao:* And in 1998 Westminster Abbey in London chose your father
as one of ten Christian martyrs of the twentieth century to be
honored. Tell me about that.

*Wang:* He was honored with a statue above the Great West
Door of the Abbey. I didn't learn about it until later. Someone
sent us a thick stack of documents. They were all written
in English. Since I was only a middle-school graduate—I
wasn't allowed to complete high school because of my father's
"counterrevolutionary activities"—I didn't understand a word
of it. In December 2002 a relative's son went to London and
took some pictures of my father's statue in front of Westminster
Abbey. We all cried when we saw them. My father had fought
against devils in those dark days and had triumphed.

*Liao:* Do you feel bitter about the past?

*Wang:* No, I don't feel bitter. As Christians, we forgive the sinner
and move on to the future. We are grateful for what we have

today. There is so much for us to do. In the mid-1960s, when my father was preaching, there were 2,795 Christians in Wuding County. In 1980, after he was "rehabilitated" by the Communist Party, the number of Christians in Wuding had grown to twelve thousand, and we now have about thirty thousand. In our society today, people's minds are entangled and chaotic. They need the words of the gospel now more than at any other time.

# Chapter 10

# THE ELDER (II)

On the last day of 2005, Dr. Sun and I left Luquan County and boarded a bus for Zehei County. A heavy fog had just lifted, and the lush vegetation on the hills was refreshing to the eye. Our bus crawled along on a narrow winding road high in the mountains, the sort of road that meandered between a deep ravine and steep cliffs. Dr. Sun said a bus laden with twenty passengers, their bags, and animals had slid into the deep ravine a few weeks before.

In the distance, a bright red dot could be seen in a fold of snow-capped Jiaozi Snow Mountain. As we moved closer, the dot evolved into a cross, a Christian cross, fixed atop a white church towering five stories over an otherwise depressing little town in Zehei County.

"Many Yi and Miao people live here," Dr. Sun said, as we wandered empty streets, watched by residents sitting or standing beneath the eaves of their seemingly identical little homes. "A lot of them are followers of Jesus."

Dr. Sun led me to one of two shops on the ground level of the church—it was a pharmacy he helped set up to serve the local residents—and made a phone call. A few minutes later, a motorbike clattered toward us, and its rider, a sun-darkened youth, gathered up our bags onto the seat behind him, and we followed him to the upper village. Dr. Sun explained that the middle village was mostly shops and small businesses; most residents lived in either the upper or lower villages, which opened out onto farmland.

We walked on paths of red dirt. On one old wall had been daubed in now-faded red paint, "All ethnic groups are treated equally." I was told it was a slogan from the 1930s and left by the passing Communist army, which was on the run from the Nationalist troops. We turned into a courtyard, and there an old couple, smiles spreading their wrinkled faces, greeted us. The man was the most venerated Christian elder in Zehei County, Zhang Yingrong, and the woman, his wife, Li Guizhi.

*Zhang Yingrong:* I was born in 1922, though I don't know the exact date because I lost my mother when I was five and my father couldn't remember. He was a church elder and devoted his life to the Lord. I became a Christian at a young age, but I didn't really understand what that meant; I read the Bible because my parents wanted me to. But at the age of sixteen, two foreign Christians came to preach in the region. I took part in a service and, with my friends, took part in a three-week Bible study camp. My heart was touched. I confessed my past sins to the Lord and committed myself to the Christian faith. My church at Salaowu recommended me for a Bible school attended by students from every ethnic group in the region—the Han, the Yi, the Lisu, the Gan, and the Dai. I studied there for three years.

*Liao Yiwu:* We visited the site of the Southwestern Theology Seminary founded by two missionaries who died there more than half a century ago. Did you know them?

*Zhang:* Yes. The man came from Australia. He was in his fifties at that time. His Chinese name was Zhang Erchang. His wife was a Canadian. I can't remember her name now. Reverend Zheng Kaiyuan from Britain was another founder. He used to run a religious school in Sichuan province. After Japan invaded northern China, he came over to Yunnan and helped found the seminary. Several months later, they moved the seminary to Salaowu. After I graduated from the Bible school, I was in the first group of students to enter the seminary. During summer holidays, I would follow my teachers around to learn how to preach.

Our county was remote and backward, quite ethnically diverse. Back then, we only had mountain paths and used horses, donkeys, and human legs to move around. To get to Kunming took twenty days; now you can do it by bus in ten hours.

I had wanted to stay in Yunnan, but a few days before graduation, the seminary received a letter from a preacher in Zhaojue County in Sichuan province. He was a doctor from London and planned to set up a medical school there, but he only spoke Mandarin and the county was in the heart of the Yi region. The Yi language and culture were quite challenging for the British doctor.

The seminary sent me and another Yi student. We worked as interpreters and taught the doctor to speak Yi. I returned home at Christmas in 1950.

*Liao:* China was under Communism then.

*Zhang:* Right before Christmas in 1949, Yunnan province was taken over by the Communists. However, Zhaojue was still under the Nationalists. As a Christian, I didn't pay much attention to politics; no matter who ruled China, people needed the guidance of the gospel. At the end of 1950, the Communist Party was too busy with regime change to worry about religion. They had just started the Land Reform Movement and had to handle armed rebellions from local secret societies and landlords. I was approaching thirty years old and married. Unfortunately, my family was classified as landlord.

*Liao:* Was your family rich?

*Zhang:* My family had five boys and two girls. I was the second
child. My eldest brother was county chief under the Nationalist
government but didn't own much land. As a seminarian, I had
nothing under my name.

*Liao:* How did you get the landlord classification?

*Zhang:* Several reasons. In those days, there weren't so many
Christians in the county. Those of us who were had mostly
inherited the faith of our parents. Our family stood out. Second,
the seminary sent me to Zhaojue County, which was under the
rule of the Nationalist army. The Communists suspected I had
been sent on a secret mission for the foreign imperialists. Third,
my eldest brother's past implicated the whole family.

*Liao:* What happened next?

*Zhang:* When the Land Reform Movement started, I still lived at the
seminary. Once my family was classified, I was dragged back to
the village and locked up with several dozen other "landlords."
At first, the job of the local Communist Party was to confiscate
and redistribute land and other assets. They didn't use much
violence. Many wealthy families buried clothing and food,
thinking they could dig them up after the campaign was over.
But the campaign became more and more violent. The buried
food and clothing was found, and those landlords were severely
punished. When they asked me to cough up money, I could
honestly say I had none. When they tried to confiscate my assets,
I could offer them nothing. They searched everywhere. They
were outraged. They even went to the seminary and brought back
my belongings, which amounted to an old quilt. I didn't even
have sheets. Officials were really upset and swore at me nonstop.
How could a landlord be so poor? They didn't believe me. They
made me kneel on the ground for three days and three nights.

Local militiamen guarded me with big sticks, and each time I fell asleep, they would beat me.

*Liao:* Were you inside a jail?

*Zhang:* No, it was out in the open. They broke some roof tiles and bricks, placing them under my knees. It rained all that time. I was soaking wet and shivering and kneeling in a puddle that rose to my thighs. I closed my eyes and prayed.

I wasn't the only one kneeling in the yard. There were a dozen more like me. We were forced to confess our "crimes." I was supposed to tell them what I had done in Sichuan province, the ulterior motive of my trip. Did I try to contact the Nationalist army there? Before the government reversed its verdict against me in the late 1970s, I had written several hundred confessions.

*[Zhang stops talking, either too tired or unwilling to continue his story; his wife continues.]*

*Li Guizhi:* After my husband was taken away, I went to stay with my parents in Salaowu. Since my family didn't own land and my parents were not connected with the Nationalist government or the church, we were not affected; we were classified as part of the revolutionary masses. All I could do was cry all day. One day someone stopped by and told me that my husband was dying. I was desperate and rushed to Zehei, which was about forty-five kilometers away. I saw him kneeling in the rain, like a ghost. I squatted in front of him, but he didn't recognize me. I was afraid his soul had gone. After I called his name a couple of times, he began to respond. I had brought boiled potatoes and fed him. A militia guy came and yelled at us. I ignored him and continued to feed my husband. The guy hit us with his stick. A potato fell to the ground. It was horrible. He had been kneeling there like that for three days and three nights without food. In the end, they kicked me out. By the time I got home, my house was guarded by

members of the Poor Peasants Association. I was not allowed to
leave my home.

At the tail end of the campaign, my husband crawled home.
The night he returned, I had been unable to sleep, and just before
dawn I heard strange scraping sounds outside. When I opened the
door, there was a person covered in mud lying at my feet, hands
reaching for my legs. It was my husband. He didn't even have the
strength to moan. I pulled him inside, wrapped him in a quilt.
Several hours later, the local militia people arrived. They wanted
to drag him to a public denunciation meeting. When they realized
that he couldn't move, they found a wooden plank and carried
him out, put him on stage, and forced him to open his eyes.

*Zhang:* There were about three to four thousand people there.
I couldn't move. There were ten others on the stage for
denunciation, all tied with ropes. My eldest brother was there
beside me, his arms held behind him by two militiamen, his body
bent to ninety degrees. I lay on the wooden plank, looking up.
The rain had stopped. Amid the loud shouting, I could hear the
river nearby. The clouds had dispersed and the sky was a clear
blue. I thought: *People lived harmoniously under this same sky in the
same village for many years. Why did they act like this now? Why did
they hate each other and torture each other like that? Was that what
the Communist revolution was all about?* All the "class enemies"
had been beaten; their faces were swollen and their heads scarred.
Beatings couldn't quench their thirst. They started killing. After
that meeting, all the former officials under the old regime were
executed, including my brother; their children were sentenced to
ten or twenty years in jail, where some lost their minds, or died.

I wasn't involved in politics at all. I had never exploited
anyone. So they let me live. The torture left me disabled for the
rest of my life. I was ordered to work under the supervision of

the revolutionary masses. I wasn't allowed to preach, of course.
In 1958 during the Great Leap Forward campaign, they sent me
to a labor camp. Around that time, our commune was building
a dam. My job was to dig mud. After that, I was assigned to a
different reeducation group and worked at a coal-burning kiln for
ten months. Our group had about 250 members; within a month,
one third had fallen ill because there wasn't enough food. We ate
soupy rice porridge every day and didn't have the strength for
heavy labor. I wasn't a strong person in the first place.

That was the summer of 1959, a year of widespread starvation.
We had eaten everything—tree bark, grass and leaves, things
animals didn't even touch. Many died of food poisoning. One day,
three in my group dropped dead by the side of a road. Passersby
stripped off their clothes. Their teeth and tongues stuck out, as
if they were still hungry. We had to bury the bodies deep or they
would be dug up again. People were desperate for anything.

*[Zhang stops talking to rest.]*

*Li Guizhi:* When he was taken away to the labor camp, our eldest
daughter was only three months old. She cried all day for food.
Eight months later, she died, and I was suffering that loss when
my cousin brought me a message: "Your husband is dying of
starvation. You'd better go save him." If he died, I did not think
I'd be able to live either. So the next morning, before dawn, I
waited outside the village chief's house. When he woke up, I went
in and knelt in front of him, begging that he lend me some grain
so I might take some food to my husband. He let me have five
kilograms and three yuan for bus fare to reach the camp. There
were bodies everywhere. One minute, you saw someone standing
in front of the coal-burning kiln; the next minute, you turned
around and the person would be lying on the ground, dead. My
husband wasn't at his dorm, so I gave someone there some of

the food I had brought with me and asked him to help me look.
I found my husband curled up in a pile of rotten grass. I had to
call his name several times and shake him before he opened his
eyes. He gobbled up some of the food and felt strong enough to
stand. Before I left, he hid the rest of the food at a secret place.
In the fall of 1959, the camp was disbanded and he returned
home. Soon after, he became paralyzed. He had rheumatism. For
three months, he couldn't move. Since he couldn't go to work
in the field, our ration was reduced, and his illness worsened. I
begged our village chief again to give us more food. The chief
discussed it with the other village officials, and in the end they let
us have some wheat, which I made into a gruel mixed with wild
vegetables to feed him each day. It was a daily struggle.

One day an herbal doctor passed by our village and heard
about my husband's illness. He had me dig a hole in my backyard
and filled it with dried mulberry leaves. Then we burned the
leaves and perched my husband on top. The smoke scorched his
body for a whole day, from sunrise to sundown. The dampness
in his body gradually leaked out. The next day, we filled the hole
with dried pine needles and did the same thing. You know what?
The remedy actually worked. Soon he could stand up but for only
a couple of minutes. Then a friend gave us a bottle of Yunnan
White Powder, which was effective against rheumatism. It was
very hard to get at that time. Thank the Lord, he finished the
meds and gradually recovered. He still can't do much heavy work
in the field but he can move about without problems.

*Zhang:* I also learned how to survive. When they needed me for
public denunciation meetings, I would be there on time. Before
they forced me to bend, I did it myself. I survived the "Four
Cleanup" and "Socialist Education" campaigns. The most

horrible campaign was the Cultural Revolution. I only have one
tooth left. The Red Guards knocked out the rest.

*Liao:* What happened after the Cultural Revolution was over?

*Zhang:* Before 1982 nobody dared worship publicly. If we
were caught, we would have to go through the same public
denunciation meetings. Gradually, Christianity spread secretly
among villages. In the past couple of years, the policy loosened
up and there has been a revival. People flocked to God in
droves, village after village. In the old days, people were fervent
supporters of Communism. Nobody believes in that now. Even
some Communist Party members have come to worship God and
confess their sins. Some even donated money to help repair our
church. In the past, I have gone through all sorts of sufferings.
Each time I was plunged into despair, I prayed and sought
guidance from the Lord. I lived through fifty years of suffering.

Throughout my whole life, I passed four tests. The first one
came when I was eight. I was herding goats on a warm autumn
day and fell asleep. When I woke up, all the goats had run away.
Worrying that my father would scold me, I burst out wailing
and attracted two wolves, which stood right behind me, ready to
snatch me away. I didn't realize they were behind me. I just kept
crying. Wolves are ferocious but suspicious animals. My nonstop
crying must have confused them. They just stood there. Then
my father arrived; he knew how to handle wolves. He cupped his
hands in front of his mouth and howled. Then the herding dogs
heard his howling and started to bark. The wolves became scared
and ran away reluctantly. That night, we found all the strayed
goats. When people heard the story, they all believed I was
protected by God.

When I was seventeen, I caught smallpox without realizing

it. On my way home one day, my body felt feverish, as if many bean sprouts were pushing through my pores. I found a small stream nearby and crawled over to drink water from it. I soon passed out. When I woke up, I noticed the red spots appearing like worms on my face and body. For the next day and half, I was in and out of consciousness. Then a dog found me and started barking, catching the attention of passersby, who carried me to a doctor's home. The doctor saved my life. If God hadn't been with me, the dog wouldn't have found me.

Then I survived the brutal beatings and recovered from my rheumatism during the Land Reform Movement, and my wife saved my life when I was dying inside the labor camp in 1959.

*Liao:* You have a good wife.

*Zhang:* When she married me, she was only seventeen, a pretty girl. She grew up in a proletariat family. In those days, she could choose any man she wanted. I saw her when my brother and I went to preach in her village. I asked a matchmaker to connect us. Luckily, she said yes. My wife suffered so much for me. At the moment, I'm fairly healthy, but she's been sick for more than seven years with rheumatism and cancer. There's no hope for a cure. Even though I'm helpless and can't share her suffering, I hope she can be comforted by the love of God. Without my wife, I would have died a long time ago. At this time, she's getting weaker and weaker. I'm getting old too. I can't share her pain. That's probably our last hurdle in life.

### Epilogue

Elder Zhang died quietly at his home on the day of the Chinese Moon Festival in 2007. He was eighty-five.

*Chapter 11*

## THE YI MINISTER

It was a scene reminiscent of the Mao era when, each night, members of our commune in rural Sichuan would gather at a courtyard house and sit around gas lamps for political study sessions or public denunciations of landlords and counterrevolutionaries or to hear the year-end income results or argue about grain distribution. Having already worked a full day in the fields, everyone was tired and many ended up dozing off.

This gathering was different; for a start, everyone was awake, alert, and eager, even enthusiastic. The local driver I had engaged as my guide said I would be attending the Eucharist and church leaders from villages in a two-hundred-kilometer radius would be present. This particular service happened once a month, moving to a different village each time, and pastors and elders would return home to deliver Holy Communion to their congregations.

The driver said it was a tremendous honor to host a multivillage service. With so many villages in the Sayingpan region, many had to compete for the opportunity. When their turns came, the host villagers would turn the occasion into a major festival. Out of curiosity, I wondered why the services were not performed inside a chapel. "I saw several white church buildings on my way here," I said.

"Services are normally conducted at individual houses," he said.

"For this, the host will slaughter pigs and chickens and prepare a banquet for every brother and sister at the service." The food would come tomorrow after morning prayers. Tonight would be more formal.

People began to sit. I found a corner, away from the makeshift stage in front of the house. I had barely sat down when three pairs of hands stretched out in front of me, one holding a cup of tea and the other two with bowls filled to the brim with soft candies and dried black watermelon seeds. I hesitated and then accepted them with gratitude.

The crowd grew thicker, knees touching knees, the smell of tobacco and garlic heavy in the air. Above us was a clear sky filled with stars and a crescent moon. The service had apparently begun, but I didn't understand the language, nor could I see who was speaking from the forest of heads in front of me. So far as I could tell, I was the only Han; everyone else was Yi, a small but distinct ethnic group within China numbering about eight million, and I was unfamiliar with their clan customs. I might as well have been in deepest, darkest Africa, rather than in a corner of my own county. But I felt quite safe, if very much alone. The voice from the stage continued uninterrupted for about an hour and a half. No one interrupted; there was no chanting or singing.

Acutely embarrassed after taking a flash photograph of the minister onstage, I slunk out of the courtyard and bumped into the driver. As he tried to explain what was being said from the stage, he stopped midsentence, took my arm, and led me to a gray-haired man who had just emerged from the common toilet. "This is Reverend Zhang Mao-en . . ." the driver said, "the person you want to interview." Zhang was the most senior clergy in the Sayingpan region; it was he who was presiding over the service.

We quickly exchanged greetings, and I pressed my case for an interview, which was not immediately confirmed. He seemed intrigued that I was working on a book about Christians in China and said, "I will see what I can do. It will probably be late. Is that okay?"

I nodded: "It's not a problem. I can wait."

"You don't have to stick around here," he said. "You've had a long day. Go stay at my house tonight. We can talk in the morning. At six? Your driver knows where I live."

I accepted Zhang's offer. It was almost two in the morning when we reached his house. Zhang's wife poured hot water into two wooden basins, and we soaked our feet. Then she led us by oil lamp to a bedroom on the second floor, where, exhausted, I dropped fully clothed onto the hard bed.

As the sound of barking dogs reached me, I opened my eyes and saw that it was morning. Zhang was not there, so we retraced our path and found him at a farmer's house, standing at a stove in a dark cavelike kitchen with his assistant. He had barely slept. They were preparing boxes of coin-shaped wafer-thin cakes and bottles of red wine for the pastors to take with them to use for celebrating the Eucharist.

We sat near the stove. His assistant, the new face of the church, retreated to a corner of the sooty room, and Zhang closed his eyes for a few minutes before indicating he was ready for my questions. It was in the early morning of August 6, 2006.

*Liao Yiwu:* When did you become a Christian?

*Zhang Mao-en:* When I was still inside my mother's womb.

*Liao:* What do you mean?

*Zhang:* My family has been Christian for ninety-two years. If my oldest brother, Zhang Run-en, were still alive, he would also be ninety-two. My father converted when Run-en was born and had him baptized. We are one of the earliest Christian families in Yunnan province. A Yi family on the other side of the Pudu River became believers even earlier. At the beginning of the last century, there was a lot of trade across the Pudu River, and preachers followed the merchants on horseback and brought the gospel to Dega, and from Dega it was taken into the mountain regions—Shengfa, Zehei, Malutang, and Salaowu.

In the early 1920s, those areas were very poor. There were no schools before the church arrived. After Japan invaded China in 1937, an Australian missionary escaped to the region and founded a seminary here. I don't know his English name, but his Chinese name was Zhang Erchang. By the time I was born, in 1939, there were a lot of Christians—my parents and siblings, my parents' parents, immediate and distant relatives, my fellow villagers rich and poor. Soon after I learned to speak, I could memorize simple hymns. The first book my parents gave me was the Bible. In remote Yi villages many people were illiterate, but you only needed to mention a certain passage from the Bible and they could recite it from memory.

Before the Communist takeover, my family was considered wealthy. My father was an elder in the church. He used to preach with Reverend Zhang Erchang. At home, he had to run the family business. My father was raised in a family with four generations of farmers. In my father's time, prices for crops had dropped and there was hardly any money made from farming. So they started raising cattle, horses, pigs, and ducks. They also raised bees. To get a better price for their animals, my family would ship their pigs and ducks to bigger markets in Jiulong and Zhuanlong. In those days, there were no trucks. My relatives would have to herd the ducks and pigs all the way down there. It normally took about ten to fifteen days. We also harvested honey twice a year and then hired porters to carry it to the provincial capital city of Kunming. We had fifty beehives. They were hard to take care of but quite profitable.

With the money we earned, my father was able to donate food and supplies to the church. Soon, the business and preaching became very exhausting for him. When I was four, he died and his brother took over.

The early 1940s was a golden age for Christianity. Our main church was in Salaowu. We had twelve pastors. There were branches in Shengfa, Pufu, Zehei, Malutang, Dasongshu, Jiaoxi, and Jiaoping. The branch in Dega was the second largest, next to the main church. My uncle became an elder in our branch. He held that position until after the Communist takeover in 1949. Then all religious activities were banned.

My oldest brother and I were both born in the year of the rabbit, but he was twenty-four years older than I. At the age of twenty, he married a woman in Pufu and moved in with his wife's family. His father-in-law was a church elder in Pufu and needed my brother's help. My brother was a graduate of the local Christian high school. He was quite smart and dedicated. He did remarkably well in the world of humans as well as the world of God. He was the county chief in Pufu and then took charge of the military draft. He used his positions within the local government to create favorable conditions for the spread of the gospel. When the church established the Southwestern Theological Seminary in Salaowu, he quit his government job and became its administrator. He personally selected every teacher and was involved in scouting and recruiting local talent. Every year, he donated more than a hundred kilograms of grain to support the preachers. All the foreign missionaries liked him.

My brother was also dedicated to social issues. Historically, the region was notorious for opium addiction. It was widespread among both the rich and the poor. On top of that, many Yi people were also addicted to gambling. These two scourges led to lots of social turbulence. Robbers and triad members ran rampant. It was a headache for every government in power. My elder brother strongly believed that the Christian faith would improve people's moral values. It would help people kick their opium and gambling addictions. He actively promoted faith as a way to cleanse social ills.

*Liao:* Your brother had a promising future . . .

*Zhang:* Unfortunately, he passed away at the age of thirty-six.

*Liao:* Did he die of illness?

*Zhang:* No. He was executed in 1951, when I was twelve. His passing left a painful memory in my family, but he left this world in dignity.

*Liao:* What happened?

*Zhang:* When the Land Reform Movement started, our family was a big target. My oldest brother's family was classified as landlords. My oldest brother and his father-in-law, the church elder, were locked up in a county jail. They were tortured. My oldest brother had served in the defeated Nationalist government, but he had a clean record. He was very well liked by local folks here. So when the new Communist government sent work teams to different villages and repeatedly mobilized people to stand out and renounce my brother, nobody was willing to do it openly. In the 1950s there was a major push to execute and eliminate members of the triad and evil landlords. My brother was spared, initially. But the government wouldn't let him go. In 1951 they threw him in the Luquan County jail and, under pressure from the government, the village officials, who used to be poor and homeless, agreed to "settle scores" with my brother.

We were not allowed to see him; we didn't know what to do to defend him. I found out later that while he was charged with crimes, they never gave details of what he had done. They had to come up with something to justify why they had locked him up for so long. I was told that a work-team leader read the charges cooked up by a local village chief, but when the leader asked for details, the village chief couldn't answer him and felt the question made him lose face, so he yelled back at the work-team leader. Since there was not enough evidence, another village official suggested that my brother be spared the death penalty, but an official at the regional level was worried that sparing my elder brother would set a bad precedent and would dampen the enthusiasm of the masses. In that era, to be a potential candidate for village leadership, all you had to do was scream loudly at public denunciation meetings and be ruthless with "class enemies."

You are too young to understand what it was like. We were treated much worse than animals. People would torture us whenever they felt like it. During the peak of the campaign, the government work teams fanned the sentiment of hatred. Even the nicest and kindest peasants began to wave their fists and slap or kick us. Toward the end, revolutionary peasants didn't need a reason to kill a landlord. At public denunciation meetings, people became carried away with their emotions and would drag someone out and shoot him on the spot. Bang, bang, and the person was gone forever. Nobody questioned this ruthless practice or took responsibility. Most of the work-team members were sent from the cities. They had no knowledge of what was going on at the local level. Chairman Mao said officials should listen to the voice of the people. And work-team members didn't dare ignore the voice of the people. Once people became brainwashed by Communist ideology and by Mao's propaganda, their thinking became chaotic. All humanity was lost. At its peak, even the work team found it hard to rein in the fanaticism.

Let me explain. In this area, it was rare to find anyone who was not addicted to opium or gambling. Only those who had

embraced God had the stamina to kick their habits. When I was
a kid, I remember that people in this area didn't grow crops.
Instead, they grew poppies. We used to run around in the poppy
fields to catch butterflies. People also gambled heavily. This was
a very strange phenomenon. People's wealth switched hands very
quickly. In the afternoon, the person might be a rich landowner.
By evening, he was homeless, having gambled everything
away—his land, his house, even his wife.

When the Communists came, they banned opium smoking and
gambling, and they banned Christianity. Apart from working in
the fields, people didn't have anything else to do in the evenings.
Political campaigns turned into a form of entertainment. They
devoted all their extra energy to beating up people, killing
people, and confiscating the property of others. Those homeless
drug addicts and gamblers suddenly became loyal revolutionary
allies. They didn't have to pay off their debts; their gambling and
drug habits, their poverty, the practice of pawning their wives
and children for drug money, their homelessness, everything was
the fault of landlords exploiting poor revolutionaries.

Poverty became a badge of honor, and the children of the poor
became the offspring of the true proletariat. They felt superior
to everyone else and were well fed and clothed. They didn't even
have to take any responsibility when killing someone at public
denunciation meetings. That was more fun than smoking opium
and gambling, don't you think?

*Liao:* In the Mao era, we say, people became the true masters of the
nation.

*Zhang:* The Communist Party's policies might have been well
meant, but the people who implemented them took a lot of
liberties and interpreted them in their own way. Random killing
was quite liberating. My oldest brother knew he wouldn't survive.

*Liao:* Were you there when your brother was killed?

*Zhang:* After my brother was imprisoned, nobody, not even his
   wife and children, knew his whereabouts. Two days before
   the execution, my family was told that my brother would be
   transferred from a jail in Luquan County to Sayingpan for one
   condemnation meeting and then to another in Shengfa Township.
   After that, he would be sent back to Pufu to be executed. If we
   wanted to see him for the last time, we had to get up at midnight
   and walk twenty kilometers to a place between Sayingpan and
   Shengfa and wait by the side of a road. So we did. The night
   before my mother left, we sat together and cried. We tried to keep
   our voices low so the neighbors wouldn't hear us. My mother
   slaughtered a chicken and cooked it with rice, and she and my
   second elder brother and my elder sister left the house. She didn't
   allow me to go for fear that it could be too traumatic for me. I was
   thirteen years old. My mother and my siblings came back the next
   evening. I asked if my oldest brother had eaten the chicken. My
   mother nodded; her eyes were all red. Over the years, my mother
   told me about her last meeting with my brother.

   They waited at the designated spot for about three hours. The
   truck carrying my brother stopped, and he got out. My mother
   begged the militiamen to take off his shackles so he could eat his
   last meal. They did. My brother ate the chicken and the soup.
   When he finished eating, he whispered to my mother:

   "I'm going to be gone soon. Don't be sad. I'm not afraid
   of death. While I was locked up in jail, I've been carrying a
   miniature Bible. I smuggled it in with me. I've been praying in
   my heart. I know that I won't be able to escape death. People in
   the region have charged me with many crimes even though they
   don't even know me. I'm innocent and their charges are false.
   I'm not going to admit guilt. But I'm not going to appeal either.

I know it's useless. They will ship me back to Pufu to have me killed there. I'm glad that I'm going back to Pufu. I have my Bible with me. I will be buried in the place where I used to work and preach. Mother, we are all going to die someday. Don't be discouraged by my death. Continue with your faith."

On the day of my brother's execution, the militiamen came and told my sister-in-law, "We are going to execute your man. Bring some nice food."

Like my mother, my sister-in-law slaughtered and cooked a chicken and some rice. My oldest brother ate it all. She was sobbing. My brother wiped away her tears and told her to follow the words of the "Leader." He told her to focus on the children and not be bothered by the taunts and insults from others.

We knew exactly what the word "Leader" meant. He didn't want to implicate his wife and say it in front of the guards. My sister-in-law understood. She stopped crying. They took him away. After a final public condemnation meeting, the militiamen shot him by the roadside and dumped his body in a shallow hole in a ravine. About ten months later, we were notified that we could collect the body. Do you know why? The ravine was pretty close to the main road and my brother's exposed corpse scared people. The county leadership decided our family should take the counterrevolutionary's body away so no one would have to look at it.

My brother's rotting corpse looked like a fallen tree stuck in a stream. My second oldest brother and my mother went down into the water to drag it out, and it fell to pieces. We collected the bones, washed them, and put them in a box we had brought with us.

My mother found his little Bible tangled up inside his rotting clothes. It was about two centimeters thick, no bigger than the palm of my hand. Though his clothes and flesh had rotted away after ten months in water at the bottom of a ravine, his Bible had survived. We all stopped what we were doing and began praying, not a formal prayer but silent prayers of thanks. God had stayed with him all those months. We knew his soul was in heaven.

*Liao:* What did the Bible look like?

*Zhang:* It was bound together with leather and string. Some of the pages had stuck together, some of the words had blurred, and there were bloodstains. We kept it for many years. But one political campaign followed another; it was hard enough preserving our lives, and the Bible was "counterrevolutionary evidence." During the Cultural Revolution, my mother burned it. She had no other choice.

We were lucky that we didn't get arrested like my oldest brother, but we were kicked out of our house. My mother, my second elder brother, and I were classified as landlords.

My sister had been married to a man in Jiaoxi region, and they were also of the landlord class. My uncle, a church elder, was labeled a counterrevolutionary landlord. All my family was in trouble. We became homeless and lived in "cowsheds." Several times when I ran into the children of peasants on the street, they would accuse me of wearing nice clothes and make me take them off. We didn't have enough to eat and were constantly the target of condemnation meetings.

If village officials were in a bad mood, they would taunt us if we encountered them on the street, or beat us up. If they were in a good mood, they would order us to do their work in the fields, even though we were weak from hunger. Each time there was a new campaign, we would be targets of persecution. My uncle underwent three hundred public condemnation meetings. His health deteriorated fast. He died in 1958 of tuberculosis.

In 1953 they reclassified my mother—we were downgraded from landlords to rich peasants and were able to get back our house, which had been seized by the village, and a small plot of land.

My second elder brother—he was twelve years older than I—was hard of hearing. He was a pious Christian. He continued his prayers all through the 1950s, when my family was suffering at the hands of the work teams. One day, he was seen on his knees praying and was reported to the work team. They ordered him to say that belief in God was superstition and counterrevolutionary. He refused to renounce his faith. Instead, he closed his eyes and kept praying. They tied his hands and feet and hung him on a tree for several days. When they cut him down, he would be on his knees again, praying for the Lord to forgive his torturers. His health declined. He contracted TB. But he persisted. Before his death in 1999, he traveled all over the region, helping and praying for the poor and the sick.

In the later years of the Cultural Revolution, I was jailed three times for secretly preaching the gospel. I suffered but survived. In 1979 the government relaxed its control over religion. From 1979 to 2003, I served as a church elder. Then I became an ordained minister in the Sayingpan region. I'm the first ordained minister in my family. Like my second oldest brother, I also suffer from TB and take all sorts of medicine. None of it has helped much. My second brother died at the age of seventy-two. I'm sixty-eight. I don't know what God has planned for me, but while I am still able, I want to try to do more. As you could see last night, more and more local people are following Jesus. It encourages me.

*Chapter 12*

## THE FEAST

Yi ballads can be boisterous and jubilant, or serene, or reminiscent of lone traveling spirits, full of sadness and melancholy. My first encounter with the Yi ballad was in a bar in 2007 when I was traveling in Dali. I met a French musician who had just returned from a trip to several Yi villages in the Daliangshan area. With his expensive recording equipment, he had collected several dozen ancient ballads and burned them onto three CDs. We drank together as he played me a selection.

Those songs entered my dream one night. A simple repetitive melody echoed inside the dark, bare mountains, every note dripping tears, as slithery as earthworms. When I woke up, my feet were ice cold, which I like to attribute to my subconscious interpretation of the Yi culture—a people coming from the dark, damp mountains, their beings a combination of gods, ghosts, and humans.

In early August 2006 I was invited by Reverend Zhang Mao-en to attend a service held not in a church but in the yard of a parishioner's house. As he led me along a narrow, muddy path that wound through the village, giving way to strolling cattle adorned with bells and clip-clopping horses with rounded bellies, I trod carefully, avoiding deep hoofprints filled with steaming dung. Zhang seemed oblivious to the petty disruptions of rural life.

The sight and smell of so much manure reminded me of an allegorical article I was made to read in high school during the Cultural Revolution. A group of urban youths sent down to the rural areas to receive "reeducation" stumble upon a pile of fresh cow dung on a similar muddy path. As they search for a shovel to scoop it up, a peasant girl appears, cups the dung in both hands, and carries it to the communal manure pond. The young peasant girl sets a powerful example for the young city people who are unable to see past their petty bourgeois habits. Our teacher left us with a series of questions: Which was worse—the horse dung or petty bourgeois thinking? Who had the purer mind—the peasant girl or the urban youths? Some forty years later, school teachers no longer imbue cow shit with Communist ideology. Chinese people know shit stinks and that anyone in his right mind would use a shovel to collect it, whether proletariat or bourgeoisie.

What should have been a five-minute walk took half an hour, and by the time we arrived, my pants and shoes were a muddy mess. I stomped my feet on dry ground, trying to shake myself clean, when the driver touched me on the shoulder and said, "Don't waste your energy. The mud will dry in no time and come off easily." As we approached the parishioner's courtyard home, I could hear hymns blasting from two Mao-era loudspeakers, very like those used by Party cadres during denunciation meetings, mixing in a painful static that drilled at my eardrums and cast me back for a moment to darker times.

The sun was well up now, and the air was humid and full of cicada song. I licked my parched lips, looked around to get my bearings, and realized it was here, the night before, that I had met Zhang. The house and the yard looked very different in daylight, the surreal and magical rendered shabby and crude, the crowd indistinguishable from any other gathering of ordinary, simple peasants, except that they were all smiling with what I can only ascribe to faith-induced happiness.

Zhang's head of silver-gray hair disappeared fast inside the house. He was the only ordained minister in the Sayingpan region, so this was his show. I watched his parishioners, and what at first glance appeared to be chaos resolved itself into order as greeters arranged seats and passed around tea and candies while the cooks chopped and clattered in the kitchen.

Christians in China's major cities are greatly divided over the government-sanctioned churches, but villagers here are not so political. They attend Sunday service at government-sponsored churches run by Zhang but also participate in services held by family pastors.

Around me in the courtyard, the talking stopped and ears strained to hear Zhang's voice as it rose and fell on the warm morning air. I listened but couldn't understand a word. He was speaking Yi. It was like listening to a tape of poet T. S. Eliot reading his poems when I was young. I could only decode the meaning from the tones and rhythms and with my eyes, my nose, and my mind. I let my imagination fill in the blanks and felt I could see the blood of Jesus, smell the fetid air before his death, and share the exultation of others around me of his resurrection. It was not a long service, and soon the crowd uttered "Amen" and life snapped back to its noisy secular state.

Language made it impossible for me to interview participants. Since many had seen me arrive with Zhang, I could move freely with my camera, trying to capture interesting faces and unusual scenes. Mounds of garbage and dirt piled up along the walls near the yard entrance. In another corner, a pigsty and a chicken coop. Animals and humans lived side by side, forming a harmonious picture. Four old ladies sat side by side on the bottom stairs of the house, facing the scorching sun. One stood up, slowly wobbling forward. I focused on her weathered face, the deeply creased forehead.

It was approaching noontime and the flies were out and about.

When the villagers around me made a gesture or laughed or shook hands in greeting, flies would rise and swirl around them. When they stopped, the flies would drop back on their heads, shoulders, arms, and legs. Little clouds of flies hovered over the more animated of conversations.

Zhang beckoned to me, and I went inside the house, where it was cooler and there were fewer flies. He introduced me to several pastors from other villages, but our conversations in Mandarin were of the simple kind and limited to common phrases. They all looked tanned, crimson like the red soil of the Yunnan-Guizhou Plateau, their faces exuding kindness and nobility. When we ran out of words, we sipped our tea and smiled at one another.

Outside, four tables were being set up for food. Growing up in the rural areas of Sichuan province, I had attended all sorts of banquets— weddings, funerals, birthday celebrations—but none quite like this one. People in Yunnan were accustomed to low benches and short tables, whereas folks in Sichuan preferred higher benches and long tables. But the banquet customs were the same. From ancient to modern times, people in every province have maintained celebratory traditions— slaughtering pigs and goats and filling big plates and bowls with me- ticulously prepared meat and vegetable dishes.

The cooks rushed in and out of the kitchen. The hostess invited Zhang and the other pastors and preachers to step out to the yard. Everyone got up and bowed to one another. "Please, you go first, I can wait." Nobody moved. A few minutes later, the hostess appeared again, urging Zhang outside. "Please, you go first, I can wait." After a third such exchange, Zhang grabbed my wrist and said to everyone, "Let's all go outside and start." Zhang led the other church leaders down the steps, waving to the crowd, exchanging a few words here and there as he headed for the tables. Each was occupied by eight to ten villagers; more lingered outside the courtyard waiting to join the second sitting.

Pork, lamb, chicken, duck, tofu, peanuts, and vegetables, stir-fried, steamed, stewed, and raw—most of the dishes looked and smelled as if they were heavily spiced with hot chili peppers. Within minutes, the table was covered by a dozen or so dishes. The sun was now overhead. I was very hungry. The flies seemed more like ravens, trying to snatch up the food. At other banquets, people would clink their glasses and toast each other with loud yelling. On this day, the courtyard was silent, save for the buzzing of flies. The mountain loomed large in the distance, glorious in the sunlight.

Zhang stood, gazed into the distance, and lowered his head to lead a prayer. He towered above us on the low benches. Every Yi word he uttered sounded melodic and beautiful.

Zhang was praying.

I felt overcome by an entirely different set of emotions. The damp solitary darkness in my dream evaporated around me. His voice, deep and thick, and the melodic words made me think of the beautiful uplifting gospel music of the American blacks or the soul-grabbing chanting of the ancient African tribes.

Zhang was praying.

As his "Amen" was chorused by everyone present, my ears returned to the normal sounds and activities of life as chopsticks began clicking through the food. More dishes were served. Zhang engaged in some lively conversations with his neighbors around the table. They laughed, openly and freely and with happiness.

At that moment, I remembered a passage from the Bible, which I had read before the trip. "On this mountain, the Lord of hosts will make for all people a feast of rich food, a feast of well-aged wines" (Isa. 25:7). It was truly a memorable feast and a celebration of life.

. . .

The feast was over by one o'clock. After I made my farewell to Reverend Zhang, my driver recommended that I visit the site of the former Southwestern Theology Seminary in Salaowu.

The car glided on a newly paved concrete road; small tractors spewed plumes of black smoke, tainting the pristine air. When the driver stopped on the edge of a cornfield, I could see the outline of the seminary, standing like a lone island among a green sea of cornstalks. I began feeling unusually animated and eager. I leapt across ditches and walked briskly. I thought of Dr. Sun who had regaled me with stories about the seminary and its founder, an Australian missionary named Zhang Erchang. In the early twentieth century, the seminary became an incubator for Christian leadership in the region. When Zhang Erchang and his wife died, they were buried nearby. Nearly all the Christian leaders I had interviewed in the region mentioned this seminary and remarked on its tremendous influence over the local Christian community. My expectations ran high as I dashed across the cornfield, with the driver calling me from behind, panting and shouting, asking me to slow down.

Two or three small drab buildings with gray roof tiles made up the whole campus. If one didn't know about its history, one would assume it was a small collection of farmhouses. There were no Western-style buildings, no stained-glass windows or biblical frescoes.

A villager directed us to the chapel, with its yellow crescent sun logo painted on a second-floor window. We followed several villagers through a small entrance. The inside was spacious, with exposed wooden beams. Paint was peeling off the ceiling. The afternoon lights filtered in through large windows. There was a dais and a blackboard on the front wall, with a red cross hanging above. Rows of long green benches could accommodate more than a hundred people.

Half a dozen villagers sat quietly inside the empty room, like diligent students who came ahead of their class to prepare for their lessons. My eyes darted around, trying to find traces of its former glory. I wandered out of the chapel, around the yard, and even climbed up a hill at the back, hoping to locate Zhang Erchang's grave or tombstone. There was nothing.

I peeked in every room in the adjacent buildings. All I could see were dust, spiders, flies, and animal droppings. A fierce-looking dog leashed with a heavy cast-iron collar lay asleep inside a dilapidated room. In another building, I ran up to the second level; the wooden floors looked moldy and rotten. I took a couple of steps forward and heard a loud crash. A big hole appeared. A small crowd gathered down on the lower level and looked up, trying to figure out what was happening.

We came down. The driver followed me closely, worrying that I would get myself into some more embarrassing troubles.

I sat despondently on a flight of stone stairs in front of the chapel. A group of people walked past me to attend an afternoon service. I stopped one pious-looking woman and asked slowly in Mandarin: "Did you know a missionary named Zhang Erchang? Do you know anything about the Southwestern Theology Seminary?"

She looked befuddled and shook her head. She had no ideas what I was mumbling.

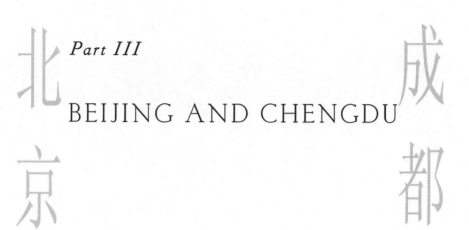

# Part III

# BEIJING AND CHENGDU

*Chapter 13*

## THE SECRET VISIT

Xu Wenli was a prominent human-rights activist, so it should have come as no surprise that it was in his cramped courtyard house on Baiguang Road in Beijing that I first encountered a member of China's underground "house church" movement. This was in July 1998 and I had stopped by my friend's house thirsty for some tea and found he had another visitor, middle aged with glasses, who was introduced to me as Xu Yonghai, a neurologist. We nodded at each other. The two Xus were not related but looked like brothers, both thin and pale skinned with long narrow faces, Wenli balding on top, Yonghai slowly losing his hair.

After the usual exchange of greetings, Wenli beckoned for me to sit and said by way of apology, "Let me just finish my conversation with Yonghai." Sitting close, the pair whispered, but I gathered from the scraps I could catch that they were planning to print some banned materials. Yonghai was tense and would, every few minutes, raise his head furtively and look outside to see if anyone was there. When they had apparently finished their business, Yonghai moved closer to me and whispered, "We have to be careful. I think Wenli's home is bugged." I nodded, acknowledging his caution.

He wanted Wenli's help with a publication for Beijing's house-church members and, warming to me, talked about the concept of salvation through God. I knew little about Christianity at the time. I was not really interested in what he had to say. Deep down I rejected his proselytizing. In the end I said, "I don't go to the church." He laughed, "I don't go to the church either . . . they are all government controlled."

Four months later, after returning to Sichuan, I learned that Wenli was given a thirteen-year prison sentence for establishing an opposition party in China. I further learned that just before Wenli's arrest, Yonghai helped remove the handwritten manuscript of my book *My Testimonials,* which I had hidden at Wenli's house, and it was now in a safer place.

Yonghai and I talked a few times over the telephone until I discovered, in 2002, that his phone had been disconnected. I sent out feelers for his contact information and discovered that the neurologist was a preacher and leader in Beijing's "house churches." After his home was targeted for demolition by a private developer, Yonghai led a residents' protest against unfair treatment, but their numerous petitions to the government for help were ignored. After his house was reduced to rubble, he considered suicide as a way to make a statement but was dissuaded by fellow Christians. I was told he had quit his medical practice and dedicated himself to following the path of God. In 2004 I read a report saying that Yonghai and another Christian, Liu Fenggang, were arrested while preaching the gospel in Zhejiang province. The government blocked any information on his whereabouts or his health. Occasionally, I would see online postings by his nurse wife, Li Shanna, who called on fellow Christians to pray for the safety of her husband. Yonghai spent three years in prison.

Curious about Yonghai's story, I decided I needed to interview a "house church" Christian to understand more of what drives them to reject the government-sanctioned alternative. I was back in Beijing in February 2004, when a preacher friend, Liu Min, called to say she had a telephone number for me if I wanted to talk to Yuan Xiangchen, a respected figure in the Christian community in Beijing. I got through to his eighty-six-year-old wife, and she agreed to meet me. I jotted down the address and instructions on how to get there by subway. Excited at this rare opportunity to talk with a Christian couple whose lives spanned much of the twentieth century, I invited a documentary maker from Taiwan, who went by the name of Ms. Wen and has made several films about social issues in her homeland, to join me.

A week later, the three of us met at the Xuanwumen subway station. Waves of dusty, cold wind from the tall gray buildings lashed at our faces relentlessly. We all flinched and instinctively clutched our hands to our chests. Before heading downstairs to the train platforms, Liu Min spotted a Catholic church on the side of the road, the pale winter sun painting a layer of gold on the cross that stood high above the church steeple. Liu suggested we go for a quick visit. Inside the spacious prayer hall, Liu knelt down on the floor for a short prayer.

We boarded the subway and got off at the Yangqiao Hospital. Liu Min, a Beijing native who was supposed to be our guide, got lost, so it took another half hour to reach our destination.

"We want to visit Uncle Yuan," Liu Min told the security guard at the building we managed to find with the help of passing strangers. "He lives on the second floor."

"Who are you?" the guard asked, but Liu Min ignored him as she hit the buzzer for 202. Ms. Wen, who didn't have much of a clue about China's tough political situation, took her video camera from her bag and started filming. Her action caught the eye of the guard. But at that moment, a departing resident opened the main door and we all slipped inside.

Reverend Yuan Xiangchen's apartment was small but comfortable. There was a cross on the wall and several calligraphic scrolls—proverbs from the Bible. A family picture above the sofa—of Yuan and his wife surrounded by more than thirty people—showed four generations of a large family, and I could identify a dozen or so faces in the relatively spacious living room. Liu introduced us and then sat down next to Yuan's wife. They had never met but acted like they had known each other for years. I felt a little uncomfortable seated next to Yuan, who had the aura of seeming to be larger than his small frame should allow. He was hard of hearing, and each time I said something, he would cup his right hand to his ear as if to catch my words. To break the tension, Liu told some stories involving her Christian activist friends and their often comical encounters with officious police. Soon everyone was laughing and at ease.

I took out my recorder and notebook, Ms. Wen set up her camera on a nearby table, and, on her signal, I began my interview by mentioning Yuan's appearance in Yuan Zhiming's documentary, *The Cross: Jesus in China*. As Yuan began to talk about his early involvement in the church, there was a knock at the door.

The air really seemed to freeze when a roomful of people tensed at the exact same moment, then it shimmered a little, like a bow in full draw. In an instant, video camera, tape recorder, and Christian reading materials all vanished like so many props in a magician's act. Yuan's eldest son crossed the room quietly and put his ear to the door. Knock, knock, knock. The son coughed and asked in a casual tone, "Who is it?"

"We are police from the local branch."

"Why, what's happened?" the son called through the door.

"Some neighbors reported three strangers with a video camera came to your house for interviews," said the voice outside.

"There is no media interview here," the son replied.

"Open the door. We are here to conduct a routine check."

Yuan's eldest son looked around the room to make sure everyone was ready and then, as if the director had just shouted "action," turned the door handle.

A uniformed police officer, who said he was in charge of the district, and a woman, who introduced herself as the new director of the street committee, were invited by Yuan to sit. The officer looked at me, Liu, and Ms. Wen. "Are you the ones who are conducting a media interview here?"

Yuan's wife said, "Nobody is doing media interviews. These are fellow Christians. They are here for a casual visit."

The officer addressed us again: "Are you all Yuan's Christian friends?"

"I'm a Christian," said Liu. "I heard that Uncle Yuan's been sick. So I stopped by for a quick visit. These two are my friends."

I nodded and said, "Yes, I'm curious about the church and want to chat with Mr. Yuan."

The officer turned to Ms. Wen: "What about you?"

Ms. Wen blushed—her Taiwan accent would be a giveaway—and quickly pointed at her throat with a finger.

"What does that mean?"

Ms. Wen opened her mouth, gesticulating with her hands, her eyes flickering behind her thick glasses.

Liu said, "She has a terrible throat infection and can't talk."

"Okay, if she can't talk . . ." the officer said to Liu, which meant he at least accepted her as speaking for all of us, "tell me what topics you are planning to discuss here."

Liu was good and turned the interrogation into a Christianity 101 lecture, from "In the beginning . . ." to the resurrection of Christ. She was a born preacher, dazzling the officer and the street committee director, both of whom looked lost. The policeman tried to stop Liu, but she never gave him a chance, so he soon gave up and let her talk. Time passed quickly, and when Liu was ready for a break, she smiled and asked the officer, "Do you have any questions?"

The policeman shook his head, but the street committee director asked, "Why do people believe in God? What good does it do us?"

The room laughed and, though flushed with embarrassment, so did she. I thought we might be safe, when the officer's phone rang. He went out. We looked at one another nervously. He soon came back, and as Liu began to answer the street committee director's question, his phone rang again. This time he returned with an older policeman, who walked in and greeted Yuan as one would greet a friend. He was the deputy director of the local branch of the Public Security Bureau. He demanded to see our identity cards. I knew Ms. Wen didn't have one, and mine was for Sichuan. "Who would walk around with his papers during daytime?" I asked, trying to sound irritated. "It's not like we are still in the era of the Cultural Revolution."

Liu produced her ID and said, "I work for an American company. Can I vouch for them?" The deputy director thought for a few minutes, handed Liu her ID card, and asked us to write down our names, phone numbers, and addresses. Ms. Wen and I put down fake names. Liu used her real name—it was a common one she shared with tens of thousands of people in Beijing.

With Liu's audience having grown by one, she simply picked up where she had left off. Our "public servants" looked attentive, nodding their heads occasionally as if they were really listening to her, so she kept preaching, but the tension was palpable. The deputy director's phone rang four times. Each time, Liu's face would become tense, her eyes involuntarily searching out mine. Ms. Wen's face remained stern and enigmatic. Yuan became impatient. Twice he asked the deputy director, "Do you have any other questions for us?" His implied message was: "Please get your butts out of here. Don't bother us anymore." But on they sat.

Stalemate.

As we made our farewells, they did too. One of Yuan's children tucked a piece of paper in my hand. We walked for a while after we left the building, glancing around like thieves, but there was no one following us, so we stopped a taxi and jumped inside. The note read, "Wait at the Catholic church near the subway station." Liu gave instructions to the driver, and we got there in good time but were startled to find, on entering the courtyard, a new Audi parked near the entrance. I'd been suspicious of new Audis since spotting a similar one outside a dissident friend's house I was visiting several days before. On that occasion, as soon as I walked in the door, several police charged out of the Audi, grabbed the door, and shoved me out. As it turned out, I didn't have to worry. We watched the Audi parked outside the church for about half an hour, when a young man in a nice suit came out and drove away.

The three of us sought shelter from the cold wind under the arched entrance to the church. I said Liu reminded me of an underground Communist character in a popular TV drama. "You faced your enemies with wit and calmness," I said, using one of its familiar clichés. Liu deadpanned. "I was scared to death," she said in a little girl voice, and we all laughed and walked around the church to keep warm. After about an hour, Yuan's second son, Yuan Fusheng, appeared, carrying a plastic shopping bag. Inside was the video camera, tape recorder, and my notebook, all wrapped in layers of old newspapers. Yuan Fusheng, looking thin and frail, had a lot of experience working with the underground church.

Yuan Fusheng gave me a telephone number so we could reschedule our interview. It was already dusk as we said our good-byes. As I walked away, I noticed the sky was full of red clouds, the color bathing everything below—the streets and cars, buildings and people.

*Chapter 14*

## THE UNDERGROUND MINISTER

Thwarted by police in my plans to interview Reverend Yuan Xiangchen, a prominent figure in the underground Christian community in Beijng, I got hold of his second son, Yuan Fusheng, on March 3, 2004. Yuan Fusheng assisted his father in ministering to Christians who refused to attend the official churches operating under government scrutiny in the capital city.

It was a necessarily covert interview conducted in the relative safety of a crowded place, in this instance a McDonald's near the Temple of Earth. We were both early and, having spotted each other, wandered separately in different directions for a while to make sure we had not been tailed. I had seen a lot of police on the streets as the National People's Congress was in session. We crossed the pedestrian bridge and went into the McDonald's, which was crowded with hamburger-loving teenagers. We found a table in a relatively quiet corner, and I got us each a Coke. I took out my tape recorder, put a napkin on top, and moved it closer to Yuan.

"It's quite tense today," Yuan whispered. "It's always the same around this time of the year. My father's been under close surveillance. I will do the interview on his behalf. My father hopes you can visit us again."

I pretended to gaze at a young couple sitting at an opposite table and nodded at his words.

"My father is now organizing a vigil for a preacher, Dr. Xu Yonghai, who was arrested while spreading the gospel in Zhejiang province. At a service not long ago, my father said Dr. Xu is a proud example for all young Christians."

I was glad to hear mention of Yonghai's name. My eyes kept moving around the restaurant, scanning faces, alert to anything out of the ordinary. And so we talked for three hours.

*Yuan Fusheng:* My father's name is Yuan Xiangchen. He was born in June 1914. He has forgotten the exact date but prefers to celebrate the day he was reborn, when he became a Christian—December 29, 1932. My father says every person should have two birthdays, one for the body and the other for the soul. My father was baptized by Reverend Wang Mingdao with the pure stream water from the Summer Palace, right behind the Wanshou Mountain.

My father was born in Bengbu City, Anhui province. My grandfather was a Guangdong native. As a young man, my grandfather worked on the construction of the Beijing-Guangdong railway and the whole family moved north with him, from Guangdong to Bengbu, and eventually settled in Beijing. My grandfather had received a Western-style education in a Chinese college, and after working with the Westerners helping to build the railway, his English was very good. So my father was born into a Westernized family. At the age of thirteen, he went to a school run by the YMCA, studied English, and memorized many passages from the Bible.

His teenage years were difficult. The constant moving by his parents left him rootless. For a while, he sank into a deep depression and attempted suicide twice by plugging a pair of scissors into an electric socket. He says two of his teachers had

a tremendous influence on him. One was an American whose
Chinese name was Xiao Anna and the other one was a Chinese,
Shi Tianmin, both of whom were pious Christians. They taught
him the new science and new social thinking advocated by Dr. Sun
Yat-sen after the fall of the Qing dynasty and the birth of the new
republic. They also spread the gospel. My father became interested
in religion and was introduced to Reverend Wang Mingdao.

In the summer of 1934, my father finished his freshman year
at a senior high school. His parents wanted him to continue with
school, graduate, and get a stable job so he could get married,
have children, and live a comfortable life. But my father resisted.
He quit school. Inspired by the Bible, he enrolled in a seminary in
Beijing. It was affiliated with the Far East College of Theology.
He studied there for four years. In the summer of 1936, he joined
two thousand other Christians and attended a national Bible
reading and consultation retreat. In 1937 he began publishing
inspirational articles and translated from English to Chinese a
handbook for preachers.

In that year, Japan invaded China. It was a chaotic time.
His future wife and my mother, Liang Huizhen, had fled her
hometown and arrived in Beijing after the Japanese occupation.
She was also a Christian, and the two met and fell in love. After
my father finished his studies at the seminary, they became
engaged and were married in Beijing in July 1938. The wedding
was half Western and half Chinese—by that I mean he wore a
suit and she wore a Western-style wedding gown, but they were
driven to the reception on a Chinese horse-drawn cart. Many
Chinese Christians and foreign missionaries attended their
wedding.

In 1939 my mother became pregnant with my eldest brother.
Around the same time, my father was asked by the dean of his

seminary to stay on as a translator, which would provide a modest
income to support his family. But he turned it down, choosing
instead to help spread the gospel in rural areas. So, with his wife
and son, he followed an American evangelical minister to preach
in southern Hebei province and parts of Shandong province.
After Japan attacked Pearl Harbor, its troops rounded up
Americans and put them in a camp in Wei County of Shandong.
One night, the Japanese soldiers took away the American
minister and his wife and two children. My father's apartment
was also looted. My mother was young and pretty and for many
months smeared soot on her face to escape being noticed by
Japanese soldiers. She and my brother hid in a cellar behind the
church.

My father, unwilling to give up, moved his family to a village
and lived and worked with farmers. The southern part of Hebei
province was under the control of Japanese troops during the
day. At night, a resistance movement organized by Communist
guerrilla forces was in full swing. My father traveled to different
villages on his bike to preach. He always carried two types of
passes and currencies, one issued by the Japanese and the other
by the Chinese Communists. Each time he ran into either party,
he would have to pay a fee in their respective currency, though
he declared himself neutral. His preaching reached a large
number of villagers. He had totally transformed himself from
an urban intellectual into a farmer—wearing black flea-infested
cotton-padded coats and eating simple wheat and corn buns.
He preached inside villages or on the side of the field. He was
so devoted that when his own father passed away, he, the only
child, didn't even have the chance to go home and say good-bye.

In 1945, on the eve of Japan's surrender, my father returned
to Beijing to take care of his mother, who was gravely ill. He

continued to preach at a church nearby and took up odd jobs
to support his family. By then, our family had grown to seven
members. My father was waiting for the situation to improve so
he could return to the countryside, where he felt he was needed
the most. However, after the Japanese troops left China, the
Communists and the Nationalists were embroiled in a civil war.
My father became restless. He prayed hard, trying to figure out
God's plan for him. During this time, he discovered a Japanese
Christian church at 160 Fuchengmen Street. The Japanese pastor
had fled China, and the Nationalist government had closed down
the church. My father was able to persuade government officials
to allow him to rent the church. The monthly rent was the
equivalent of 150 kilograms of rice. He took odd jobs to provide
financial support for the church and his family. In a way, it was a
blessing. The experience strengthened his ability as an organizer
as well as his independent spirit. He turned down any help from
government organizations, insisting that the church should be a
holy place supported by God's followers.

In late 1948, as the Nationalist troops were on the verge of
defeat, the situation in Beijing deteriorated. Many missionaries
and Christians left China. My father decided to stay. On
February 3, 1949, Communist troops entered Beijing and paraded
past his church on Fuchengmen. Three weeks later, leaders of the
various Christian denominations met to discuss how to survive
under an atheist government. At the meeting, my father urged
calm, because the Communists had announced that people could
enjoy freedom of religion. He also believed that religion should
be kept separate from secular politics. He used to tell us, "Chinese
Christians should have our own independent church. We should
move in the direction of self-reliance."

At the beginning, the new government was busy keeping order

and building support among all sectors of society. The religious sector was allowed to operate without disruption. One day my father led several of his followers on the street. They beat drums and gongs to attract people to his church. Soon he drew a large crowd. He also caught the attention of Communist soldiers who were patrolling the streets. The soldiers dispersed the crowd and took my father to the Military Control Commission. They interrogated him briefly. He cited the government's "freedom of religion" policy as defense. When he argued with his interrogators, they told him politely, "You can certainly enjoy your freedom. We have just taken over and liberated the city. There is chaos everywhere. People with all backgrounds are floating around. You shouldn't preach outside." In the end, the military leader let him go without giving him any trouble.

Within the Communist Party, there was an internal policy at that time to restrict religious activities, reform followers, and eventually wipe out all religious practices in China. In the world of religion, not everyone was as holy as he or she claimed to be.

*Liao Yiwu:* You are referring to Wu Yaozong?

*Yuan:* Yes, I'm referring to Mr. Wu, as well as other religious celebrities such as Ding Guangxun and Liu Liangmo. Let me give you some brief background information on Wu Yaozong. He was born in 1893 and became a Christian at an early age. He studied at a seminary in New York City before returning to China as an ordained minister. When the Communists took over China, he became a big supporter and accepted the Communist ideology. He said he had experienced two major transformations in life: the first was to accept Christianity as his faith, changing from an atheist into a man of belief; the second was his acceptance of the Marxist social theories, which were antireligion. He unabashedly mixed his religious beliefs with atheist Communist ideology.

Wu was elected as a member of the National Committee of the Chinese People's Political Consultative Conference. He met with Chinese Premier Zhou Enlai three times to map out the strategies for reforming Christianity in China. His plan was to sever all ties with "foreign imperialists" and to adopt the principles of self-governance, self-support—that is, free from foreign financial support—and self-propagation, which meant indigenous missionary work. These are the Three-Self principles. Soon after Wu's plan was made public, China joined a war against the Americans in Korea. The Three-Self principles quickly turned into a patriotic movement. All Christians in China had to choose between "supporting their own country" and "supporting foreign imperialists." It became fanatical. If you did not openly express your patriotism, you were a counterrevolutionary. About thirty-three thousand Christians in China signed up to support the so-called Three-Self Patriotic Movement.

Despite the political pressure, many Christians stood firm and rejected the Three-Self principles. At that time, there were about sixty Christian churches and organizations in Beijing. Leaders representing eleven churches openly aired their disagreement, saying that churches in China had long adopted the principles of self-governance, self-support, and self-propagation. There was no need to sign up again. Those brave church leaders included my father's friend Wang Mingdao.

My father wasn't among the outspoken leaders, but he had long maintained that there should be separation of church and politics. His favorite phrase used to be: let God take care of his affairs, and Caesar tend to his. Our church shouldn't be used to advance the interests of the Communist Party. His position alienated him from many of his followers, many of whom deserted him.

Starting in 1952, government officials constantly came to engage him in talks, pressuring him to join their camp. My father rejected their requests and refused to participate in political study sessions.

At first, officials at the local religious-affairs office would visit, trying to persuade him to change. They acted a bit like those police officers at our home the other day. By 1955 the government's tolerance ended. It turned out to be the largest calamity since the Boxer Rebellion in 1900, when more than twenty thousand Christians were murdered. In 1955 more than a thousand churches in China were burned down. Tens of thousands of Christians were arrested. Several thousand were executed on charges of belonging to a cult. In Beijing, the government thought rebellious religious leaders would be intimidated by what was happening in other parts of the country. Chairman Mao called this "encircling your enemies."

*Liao:* Yet no one stepped forward to support the Three-Self movement?

*Yuan:* That is correct. On the night of August 7, 1955, Reverend Wang Mingdao and his wife were arrested, along with dozens of other preachers.

*Liao:* Those church leaders got long jail sentences.

*Yuan:* From fifteen years to life imprisonment. Under threat of physical torture, Reverend Wang wrote a confession and was released immediately, but he was haunted by his betrayal. Spiritual torture was more painful than physical torture, so he turned himself in to the police. He said, "I'm going to spend the rest of my time in jail so I can appease the wrath of the Lord."

My father wavered too. Following the August 7 arrests, many preachers, including my father, bowed to pressure and took part in political study sessions. One Communist official told my father, "You are still young and have a bright future in front of you.

You should try to reform yourself." He encouraged my father
to openly express his support for the Party's policies at meetings,
but my father chose to remain silent. Deep down, he was torn.
Eventually, through prayers and self-reflection, he made up his
mind, and in 1957, when called upon to declare his support for the
Three-Self principles, he said the government's religious policy
was unfair. Freedom of religion was guaranteed in the Chinese
Constitution, but Christians could no longer enjoy that freedom.
Some Christians, the favorites of the new government, espoused
the Three-Self principles, but they were hypocrites. When the
Japanese came, they surrendered to the invaders. When the
Americans came, they managed to get on their payrolls. Now,
they ingratiated themselves to the new government. Those people
were not patriotic. They were simply opportunists who took
advantage of religion to serve their own interests. Afterward,
Father said he had never felt so elated and liberated.

During the Anti-Rightist Campaign in 1957, study groups
were told that the government required each of them to identify
four "Rightists"—people who had strayed from the Party line.
Just like that, my father had become an enemy of the people.

However, once my father was declared a Rightist, he didn't
have to pretend to be politically progressive and stopped
attending political study sessions. He stayed at home and kept up
with his routine of prayer and Bible study. He preached. "The
head of the church is Jesus, not an official at the religious affairs
office," he said when friends urged caution. Pastor Qi, an old
friend of the family, told my father at dinner with us:

"Brother Yuan, I want to offer you some advice. I know
you won't listen, but as a friend, I feel obligated to say it. You
are in a very precarious situation now. Under this new roof, I
advise you to bend your head and control your own temper. If

you can't, you should at least pretend to be compliant and keep attending political study sessions. If you continue to be stubborn and stick with your own views, you could face unimaginable consequences. Just do it for the sake of your family. You have to take care of your ailing mother and your children. If anything happens to you, what do you expect them to do? Your children will carry the black label of a counterrevolutionary for the rest of their lives. It's not fair to them."

Pastor Qi became emotional as he talked. Tears slipped down his face. My father was not moved. In the end, Pastor Qi said, "If the Communists require us to support the Three-Self policies, we have to do it. What choices do we have?"

At the end of 1957, the government reached out to my family one last time to "save" my father. A director at the local Public Security Bureau called my mother, asking her and my grandmother to show up at the local religious-affairs office. When they arrived, the deputy director greeted them with some harsh advice: "I've invited you over with the hope that you could talk with Yuan Xiangchen and change his mind. Like the Chinese saying goes, 'Rein in the horse at the edge of a cliff.' We can't put up with his difficult attitude any longer. He is still young, only forty-four years old. You should assist the government in rescuing him. Don't mistake our benevolence for weakness. If we want to lock him up, we can, in an instant. When that happens, your whole family will suffer."

*Liao:* "Rein in the horse . . ." was used during the Cultural Revolution as an ultimatum.

*Yuan:* My father knew immediately what those words meant.

*Liao:* Couldn't your father make some concessions for the sake of his family? There was no justification for your father to put his family through such suffering.

*Yuan:* He had thought carefully about such questions. He had also taken counsel from many friends. But the biggest misfortune for a Christian does not lie in the calamity that befalls him in this world. It is the betrayal of God for the sake of secular things on earth. Even if you are able to protect your relatives or your material possessions, your soul will forever be locked in darkness, without any prospect of salvation. My father believed that was the most terrible calamity.

*Liao:* I was in jail for a long time, but I still can't see myself as determined as your father. If the authorities had used my relatives and friends as hostages to threaten me, forcing me to give up my faith, I would have written confessions, lied, done whatever was needed.

*Yuan:* But you wouldn't chop off your right hand and swear never to write again, would you?

*Liao:* Of course not.

*Yuan:* It's the same principle. My father would not betray his faith, because it was his life. When a person loses his life, then what does he have left for his family?

In those long sleepless nights, my father would kneel and pray for courage. He faced two paths: he could express his willingness to change and join the government's Three-Self church, or he could accept imprisonment and separation from his family.

My father prayed for ten days, during which time no one came to bother him. He started to think that the government might change its mind about arresting him. At about eleven o'clock on the night of April 19, 1958, police came for my father. They knocked politely on the door first. Two policemen from the local ward stood outside. They "invited" my father for a quick meeting at the local Public Security Bureau office. There, several policemen were waiting for him. They read his arrest warrant and handcuffed him. He was charged with being "an active counterrevolutionary." At the same time, a group of soldiers ransacked our house, sweeping copies of the Bible, hymnals, and other Christian reading material onto the floor and trampling them. They opened and emptied trunks, went through every cupboard. With iron bars, they searched for hiding places under the wooden floor and in the walls, tearing out sections whenever they heard a hollow sound. They even scoured the pond used for baptism rituals. They found nothing out of the ordinary for a preacher; no gold nuggets, no anti-Communist materials. At four-thirty in the morning, the soldiers left with a truckload of books and everything of any value. We children stood and watched. I shall never forget that night.

My father did not come home again for twenty-one years and eight months. Mother, now the wife of an active counterrevolutionary, was stripped of her job as street committee director. My seventeen-year-old brother, who had been elected leader of a Communist youth organization, was removed from that position at school. My family was forced out of Fuchengmen Street, and eight of us crammed into a tiny fifteen-square-meter house on Baitasinei Street, ironically part of what used to be the west wing of a Tibetan lama's residence near the White Tower Temple.

To support the family, my mother went out and got a temporary job at a construction site. It was a hard-labor job that nobody else wanted. My mother was grateful for any job, even though it hardly paid anything.

*Liao:* Between 1955 and 1958, Christian ministers were arrested and churches nationwide were closed down. In Beijing, more than sixty churches were combined into four, and those four were shut

down in the Cultural Revolution. In a way, the government got
what it wanted, the elimination of all religious activities in China.

*Yuan:* But they could not control what is in people's hearts. In
those difficult years, we would join our mother in prayer every
day. One day, my mother couldn't find anything to feed her six
children. She knelt and prayed, "God, we don't have rice. We
don't have flour. We don't have anything to eat. It's going to be
like this tomorrow. If you think we should suffer like this, we will
accept it. I will feed them with hot water . . ."

The next day, a woman came to our door. "Is this Brother
Yuan's home?" she asked. My mother nodded. The woman
took an envelope from her pocket and handed it to my mother.
Inside the envelope was fifty yuan. Mother looked up to thank
the woman, but she had gone. Fifty yuan was enough to feed
the family for two months. Mother knelt and offered her thanks
to God. Over the next two decades, we regularly received
anonymous cash in the mail.

*Liao:* When did you learn your father's fate?

*Yuan:* We had no news of his whereabouts until November 1958,
when a clerk from the local court came to our house and handed
my mother a copy of the court's verdict. We learned that he had
gotten life imprisonment. When facing persecution from secular
authorities, Christians never appeal. So my mother followed this
tradition. It would have been futile anyway.

In December my father sent a postcard to us from a prison in
Beijing, indicating the date of our first allowed family visit. So
my mother brought me, my youngest sister, and my grandmother
to Zixing Road.

The waiting room was packed with visitors. Small groups
were allowed in for thirty minutes at a time. Father's head had

been shaved and he looked feeble. We were so excited to see each other. We simply held hands and didn't know what to say. My mother meant to tell him that more Christian brothers and sisters had been arrested, but a guard stood by our side throughout the visit.

*Liao:* Did your father meet any fellow Christians in prison?

*Yuan:* Yes. One night in 1959, the prisoners were watching a propaganda film outside, when he noticed that sitting in front of him was his mentor, Reverend Wang Mingdao. They looked at each other for a few seconds. Neither said anything, but they both looked up at the sky—referring to their Lord in heaven.

Sometimes, my father might run into a Christian he knew, but he became very cautious. While he was at a detention center, a former Catholic reported to the authorities that my father continued to preach during incarceration. He was punished.

At the end of summer in 1960, there was famine in many parts of China and crime rates went up dramatically. Prisons in Beijing were overcrowded. So the government decided to send prisoners with long sentences to the labor camps in Xingkaihu, in the northeastern province of Heilongjiang, along the border with the then Soviet Union. My father was one of them.

When they first arrived, they slept in tents fenced in with barbed wire and made bricks to build their own prison, after which they slept side by side in dormitories on a single fifty-meter-long bed.

In the winter, the temperature in Heilongjiang dropped to minus thirty degrees centigrade. While working in the field one day, a fellow prisoner noticed that my father's nose looked discolored. Father ran inside to warm up and was spared any serious damage to his nose. Some people, who were not as fortunate, lost their ears in the cold. Father had seen several prisoners frozen to death, like bare tree trunks in the field. It's hard to imagine how my father, a thin and physically feeble intellectual, managed to live through the long cold winters. He said he never got sick. In 1962 China and the Soviet Union officially ended their friendship and prepared for war against each other. The camps were closed. Among the more than two thousand prisoners, fifty were counterrevolutionaries—the most dangerous of criminals—and they were sent to Beijing. My father considered that to be a blessing. He would be able to see his family and the food would be better. In Heilongjiang, prisoners got by on bread made of corn chaff or wild vegetables. In Beijing, he could at least have sweet potatoes. Families could also send extra food to supplement the meager prison ration.

In October 1965 I graduated from high school and was assigned to a military farm in the northwestern province of Ningxia. Before I left, I visited Father. He grabbed my hands and held them for a long time. "You are eighteen already and will start a new life in the countryside. You should learn to take care of yourself. Are you confident about your faith? Do you know how to sing hymns?" When I answered yes to all of his questions, he smiled. I could tell he was very happy. I didn't see him again for fourteen years.

*Liao:* How did the guards treat his religious belief?

*Yuan:* The guards were indoctrinated with Communist ideology. In their minds, there was no difference between religion and superstition. Monks and preachers were the same as witches and shamans. One day, a prison officer handed out some pamphlets on how to eliminate superstitious practices in China. My father stood up after receiving the material and said, "I don't engage in any superstitious practices. My faith is true." Those around him grew nervous. But the prison officer was curious: "You claim that you have true faith. Monks in temples are considered authentic believers of Buddhism. Were you a monk?" My father answered in a serious tone, "No, I wasn't a monk in a native Chinese temple. If you really want to use a monk as a reference, I will say I'm a monk with hair in a foreign temple." The prison officer burst out laughing, and after that my father's nickname was "foreign monk."

*Liao:* That officer seemed to be open-minded.

*Yuan:* Compared with those in other provinces, prison officers in Beijing were much more educated and civilized. Conditions were also better. But the good days didn't last long. In 1966, the Cultural Revolution started and many intellectuals and former government officials were branded counterrevolutionaries. Within a short time, prisons in Beijing were full and the authorities again relocated prisoners with long sentences to Heilongjiang. My father was sent to a different farm. They had to start all over again—making bricks, building new dorms. By the end of 1966, even prisoners were mobilized for the Cultural Revolution and were told to expose each other's anti-Party thinking and activities. My father was a "lackey of the foreign imperialists" and transferred to a jail for stricter supervision, which meant he had to attend political study sessions every day, listen to political speeches, and write confessions. In the area of politics, my father was an illiterate. Even though he sat through many political study sessions, his mind was elsewhere. He never paid attention. One day he was listening to a news broadcast with a group of prisoners when, absentmindedly, he wondered out loud, "How come we never hear President Liu Shaoqi in our daily newscast? Has he lost his position? Does it mean there is political infighting within the Communist Party?"

Liu Shaoqi had been purged by Mao, and my father's remarks were reported. He was accused of "harboring evil intentions" against the Party. During interrogation, he kept his answers short: "Yuan Xiangchen, do you still believe in God?" "Yes, I do." The officer thought he had heard it wrong. He repeated the question, and my father said calmly, "Yes, I do." The officer became furious. "You are a damn obstinate, incorrigible, and extreme counterrevolutionary. Your problem can no longer be resolved through study sessions. You deserve severe punishment."

My father was locked up in a small, dark cell, measuring about two meters long and two meters wide. There was no window and no ventilation. My father said it was like being sealed in a grave. Twice a day, someone would push food through a small opening at the bottom of the door, the "dog feeding hole." My father lived in there for six months. He was ordered to sit, back straight, and reflect on his mistakes. He was monitored by the guards. If he did not sit straight, they would beat him.

As the political situation deteriorated outside, more people were purged and thrown in jail, and the prisons grew quite overcrowded. In order to accommodate the rising number of "bad" people, the prison forced my father to sometimes share his tiny cell with another inmate, but most were only being given extra punishment for a few days and would soon leave. My father was a permanent resident.

He was in the cell for six months—six months without washing, without a change of clothes, without seeing the sun— and when he emerged, he looked like a skeleton, filthy and so weak he could barely walk. When he stood up, the floor was showered with fleas. Sunlight blinded him for a long time. But he slowly recovered.

*Liao:* When I saw your father the other day, I couldn't believe that
he was almost ninety. His hair remains dark, and he looks strong
and energetic. He bears no mark of having suffered so much.

*Yuan:* His longevity and good health are much commented upon.
This may sound strange, but his jail sentence actually sheltered
him from more severe persecution in Beijing. During the
Cultural Revolution, many pastors were beaten to death by the
Red Guards. Beijing was at the center of the turmoil. Luckily, the
situation in the northeast wasn't as intense.

In the spring of 1969, my father's jail was overcrowded, so he
and other serious offenders, about a thousand prisoners, were sent
to the remote Nenjiang region. Again, they built their own dorms
and resettled.

*Liao:* How many times did he have to build his own prison?

*Yuan:* That was his fourth time. Soon after he arrived at his new
place, he ran into an old friend, Wu Mujia, one of the eleven
church leaders who refused to endorse the Three-Self policy. Wu
was serving a fifteen-year sentence. My father spotted him when
he was working in a vegetable field. The prison rules forbade
inmates talking to each other. So my father began to hum loudly
a hymn as a way of greeting. Wu heard the tune, looked up,
and recognized my father. They stared at each other for a few
seconds, and then Wu turned away. My father thought that Wu
would join him in humming the hymn. But Wu did not, and my
father was shocked by his friend's reaction. The two of them used
to be friends and had gone through a lot in life. My father later
found out that Wu had given up his faith. That news made my
father quite despondent.

*Liao:* Wasn't it the case, though, that while some caved in under
political pressure, more became determined to endure? I

remember a Christian preacher with the name of Ba Fo in the northwestern city of Yinchuan who was jailed for many years. When Chairman Mao died, he was released ahead of schedule. In his release papers, the authorities claimed that he had confessed to his crimes. He had not, and Ba Fo wanted them to correct the record. "You don't have to release me. I've never confessed my crimes." His request was rejected, so Ba Fo asked to be sent back to jail. They refused. So he built a small shed outside the prison and lived there, fasting five days a week to appease what he called the wrath of God. He lived inside the shed for twenty-some years before his death.

*Yuan:* My father's belief sustained him spiritually, enabling him to live on. None of his family members thought he would survive. Under normal circumstances, many people who got life imprisonment would end up either committing suicide or going crazy. My father underwent terrible physical tortures, but he survived. He even jokes that he should be thankful. At a labor camp in the northwest he had to carry baskets of dirt balanced at the ends of a pole, but the roads were icy and he had to keep his back straight or he'd fall flat on his face. Now he walks with a straight back, rather than hunched over, and he doesn't suffer shortness of breath, unlike other people his age.

On December 20, 1979, after Father came back from the field, an officer came into his dorm and handed him a sheet of paper, which said: "Criminal Yuan Xiangchen has been granted parole. During the parole period, which starts from the date of his release to 1989, he shall not leave his residence in Beijing. Yuan shall report regularly his activities and his thinking to the local public security bureau." With the parole paper in hand, he packed immediately and walked three kilometers to the bus stop, caught a train at the next town, crossed three provinces, and arrived in Beijing. His telegram saying he was coming home had been a complete surprise.

My eldest brother had written to the local court, saying that my father had been wrongly accused by the fanatics in the Mao era and asking the judge to follow government policy and reverse my father's verdict and clear his name. My brother was told that Father was the ringleader of a counterrevolutionary clique and the verdict would stand. He was given a form letter stating: "We have carefully reviewed your request. We believe that the original verdict reached by our court against your father still stands. The charges against him remain unchanged." The letter, dated November 16, 1979, bore the court's stamp.

*Liao:* And barely a month after that, your father is out on parole . . .

*Yuan:* The Communist Party can be capricious.

We were all at the station to meet him, but, eager to get home, he didn't linger and took a late night bus at the Baitasi stop. He walked around the neighborhood, trying to find our house, and began shouting my mother's name. My sister-in-law was home and heard my father call. It was the first time they met. By the time we got home, Father was soaking his feet in a basin of hot water.

*Liao:* How did your father adjust himself to life outside prison?

*Yuan:* It wasn't easy. He was completely out of touch with the realities of modern life, but while he had to reconnect with the physical, he remained in tune with the spiritual. If anything, his faith had grown stronger. After 1979 many people who had been jailed for religious beliefs were released. If they openly expressed support for the government-sanctioned Three-Self churches, the Religious Affairs Bureau would assign them jobs, offer them compensation, and allocate housing. Wu Mujia joined

a Three-Self church and got a teaching job at the Yanjing
Theology Academy. He lived a very comfortable life. My father
didn't even bother to ask the court to clear his name and soon
resumed his religious activities.

He turned our house into a church. Initially, he preached to
ten people at our house. Within a few years, his congregation
was three hundred and his house church was the biggest in
Beijing. Our house was certainly too small to accommodate such
a number—we would dismantle our beds to make more room—
and soon the whole alley was packed with followers when he
preached. We used to have a joke: "We are short of everything
at home, except Bibles and benches, and we were given those."
My father still holds that the government and the church should
be separate and that the church should also be self-sustaining.
Several foreign Christian organizations such as Open Doors
have offered help by donating Bibles. Father doesn't believe his
house church should be registered as a nonprofit organization as
that would place him under government authority. Our house
has been ransacked several times, and we are being constantly
harassed, but my father's position remains unchanged. He
continues to preach and the number of his followers has increased
many times over. Several years ago, we moved into a new
apartment. That was the one you visited.

*Liao:* I decided to visit your parents because I saw them interviewed
in a recent documentary film, *The Cross: Jesus in China*. There is
a scene where your father sang a hymn in his hoarse but excited
voice on camera: "So I'll cherish the old rugged cross / Till my
trophies at last I lay down / I will cling to the old rugged cross
/ And exchange it some day for a crown." With your mother
humming along, he waved his arms in the air and his face exuded
excitement. It was hard to believe that he was approaching ninety

and that he had been locked up in jail for so long. It was very touching.

*Yuan:* The name of the hymn is "The Old Rugged Cross." My parents are young at heart. I should mention the night of June 3, 1989, when fully-armed soldiers took over the streets and began their crackdown on the student protests. We could hear nonstop gunfire from our house. My father was not intimidated. He insisted that church services should go ahead without any interruption. The next morning, he got up at five o'clock. There was no bus service, so he biked fifteen kilometers to my sister's house and preached to Christians there. During the sermon, he condemned the government's action against students and citizens. He invoked the Word of God to console victims of the massacre. Looking back, it was quite scary for him to travel alone that day. There was still random shooting by soldiers on the streets, but my father, who was already in his eighties, went out calmly and fearlessly.

*Liao:* What's the government reaction to your father's activities now?

*Yuan:* We get harassed all the time. Every year, the police will accuse my father of organizing illegal gatherings and threaten to put him in prison again. The frequency of police harassment tends to coincide with the political situation in Beijing. For example, when the Party Congress or the legislature is in session, or during the anniversary of the Tiananmen Massacre, or on National Day, or when heads of state from major countries visit China, we will be under round-the-clock police surveillance. Our home phone will be tapped, or cut off altogether. They make it hard for fellow Christians to gather and hear my father's sermons. If President Obama or heads of religious or international human-rights organization visit China, the police will take my parents away and put them in a hotel somewhere to make sure my father doesn't talk with foreign media or do anything that could embarrass the government. Other times, we are okay.

*Liao:* I think many dissidents in Beijing get similar treatment.

*Yuan:* Unlike other dissidents' activities, my father's action is not intended to be antigovernment. He is here to do God's work.

*Liao:* How does your father handle this harassment?

*Yuan:* Years of incarceration haven't changed him a bit. Actually, he is becoming tougher and more determined. Each time the police show up at our house, he will step forward and confront them. "If my fellow Christians want to come, I can't stop them unless you put a padlock on my house and arrest me. I'm a person with faith. When the country's religious law contravenes my faith, I'm sorry that I have to follow the Word of God." Often, police officers can only shake their heads. As you can see, my father refuses to be swayed by secular power.

*Liao:* I heard that U.S. president Bill Clinton once invited your father to participate in an annual White House Prayer Breakfast attended by Christian leaders from around the world.

*Yuan:* Yes, but my father turned down the invitation because the U.S. government had also invited leaders of China's Three-Self churches. He had no intention of praying in the same room with those who bowed to power and gave up their faith. In addition, he didn't want to attend religious activities organized by the government, be it the United States or China. Last, even if he had accepted the invitation, the Chinese government wouldn't have issued him a passport. My father doesn't feel compelled to ally himself with money and power. It's not easy nowadays, but our whole family rallies around him. We are all Christians and, despite the challenges, I think the future looks bright here in China.

Epilogue

Reverend Yuan Xiangchen passed away in 2005 at the age of ninety-two. He had six children, all of whom are pious Christians. His son, Yuan Fusheng, whom I interviewed for this story, continues to be active in the Christian community in Beijing.

*Chapter 15*

## THE POET AND THE PRIEST

I am desperate," she whispered. "I cannot stay in China anymore. I want to escape." When I last saw Liu Shengshi, she was young and beautiful; now, her skin was weathered and rough, her forehead scored with deep creases. The leader of the avant-garde poetry movement in Sichuan in the 1980s, Liu had dropped out of sight, disappeared—no one had heard from her in years. Seeing her dressed in black and coming toward me as I sat with friends outside the Three-One Bookstore in Chengdu in 2002 startled me, as did her words. We moved to a separate table. She began to cry. She had become a Catholic activist and had been jailed for seven months for proselytizing in rural areas.

Liu had me worried, so I made some inquiries on her behalf, but when I tried to set up a meeting, she didn't return my calls and I had no other contact information for her. I saw her again three months later. It was the third day after the Chinese New Year. She was giving a talk at an outdoor teahouse. She looked calm and relaxed. "My daily prayers have given me much internal peace," she said. Liu said she was gathering information on Father Zhang Gangyi, a key figure in the Chinese Catholic community.

Liu came from a family of Communist officials. Her father had fought with Mao Zedong during the Chinese civil war. He was there when the Nationalists fled to Taiwan and he helped establish the new government in Chengdu. For years, her father took charge of the Communist Youth League in Chengdu. He met Liu's mother during the campaign to nationalize China's private enterprises. She was a worker in a textile factory and devoted to the Communist cause. They married. Liu was born in the spring of 1961, a time of famine in China when very few babies survived.

>
> *Liu Shengshi:* I was a rebel, a black sheep. I didn't have anything in common with my parents. As a child, only eighteen months old, I was sent by my parents to a kindergarten specifically for the children of senior government officials. I went to a special high school and then college. I was duck-fed Communist ideology. My parents were more dedicated to their work than to their family. When they visited me and my siblings, it was like a prison visit—short and formal. After they retired, the Party no longer needed them, and they discovered they had no life outside the Party. They didn't even know how to live together as a family. My parents are both in their seventies, but they fight all day long. They become very irrational and verbally attack each other as if they were sworn enemies.
>
> *Liao Yiwu:* They had put their faith in Communism . . .
>
> *Liu:* . . . and their faith amounted to nothing. They devoted their lives to the Communist Party, and the Party wrote them a big check, but they can never cash it because the Party is bankrupt. Several generations of Chinese have been deceived by the Party. They all became fanatics. Many former officials were attracted to the practice of Falun Gong, and no matter how hard the Party tried, they couldn't keep them from joining what the government declared was a cult. The reason was simple. Those practitioners were disillusioned with the Party. They had devoted their lives

to that promised check, only to discover it was not worth the
paper on which it was written. When my father mentions the
top Communist leaders now, it is always with a volley of curses.
He and other war veterans planned to gather in Tiananmen
Square for a sit-in demonstration. They planned to don their
uniforms, put on all their medals, and protest against the loss of
old revolutionary traditions and values. They felt that the Party's
image had been tarnished by the new leadership. The police got
wind of it and tried to talk them out of their plan, consoling them,
promising benefits. My father got into a big debate with police
officers and said afterward that it made him feel the government
was paying attention to their grievances. The veterans backed
down. They got nothing but words.

   I was fed up with my parents and their ideology. That was why
I sought a spiritual rebirth in the church. When I was baptized,
I even changed my name. My current name was given to me by
Father Zhang Gangyi. It took me a while before I found my path.
God changed my fate and I found meaning in life. It's not easy. I
was married once and strayed for a long time.

*Liao:* Don't forget that I was a friend of your ex-husband.

*Liu:* How can I forget? When we lived on Reincarnation Lane,
we tried writing stream-of-consciousness poems together.
Remember we got so drunk? We turned on the tape recorder
and talked gibberish into the microphone. We thought we were
creating the most remarkable poetry. Only one line emerged
from that experience: "A red wolf soaked in wine, his mouth
dripping." In 1986 when avant-garde poems took the country by
storm, my home became a hotel—one group of crazies moving
out, another waiting to move in. They slept all over the place,
eating, drinking, and shitting in my house. I became a full-time
cook, buying groceries and liquor. I just cooked and cooked. One

night, I locked myself up in my kitchen and turned the gas on,
trying to kill myself.

*Liao:* Why?

*Liu:* Those artist friends of mine were supposed to be the cultural
elite, but they were a bunch of soulless good-for-nothing animals.
One time, I saw them getting drunk and engaging in group
sex. It was disgusting. Where was the artistic vision in that?
Everything became so meaningless. I started to hear voices . . .

In 1989 I was teaching at a university, and when the student
movement started, I became excited and saw hope for China. I
offered a lot of support to my students. But then the government
crackdown happened. I became seriously depressed. I stopped
socializing, broke off contact with my poet friends. I would
aimlessly wander the streets. One Sunday morning, I passed the
Catholic church on Zouma Street. I could hear singing and, out of
curiosity, went in and saw hundreds of people under that beautiful
high-arched ceiling singing along with the choir and the organ.
I stood at the back, with my head down, and soon realized I was
humming along with them. I felt someone touch my elbow. An
old woman was smiling at me. Her face was creased like the bark
of a thousand-year-old tree. She gestured for me to lift my head
and sing. I felt embarrassed. I had never heard hymn singing
before. I had never heard such pure and heavenly music. Tears
welled up in my eyes. That old grandma handed me her hymn
book. When she smiled again, I noticed that she had only one
tooth left. She stood there, sticking out her dry, flat chest and
singing her heart out. The whole church was under the spell of
Jesus, not a shred of distraction. Everything was so bright and
pure. I'll never forget the first hymn that I sang:

*The Lord is my shepherd; I shall not want.*
*He maketh me to lie down in green pastures:*
*He leadeth me beside the still waters.*
*He restoreth my soul:*
*He leadeth me in the paths of righteousness for his name's sake.*
*Yea, though I walk through the valley of the shadow of death,*
*I will fear no evil: for thou art with me . . .*

I didn't dare sing too loudly, for fear I would spoil the harmony. I was possessed with happiness, like a strayed child who found her path. I looked up at the cross above the altar and at Jesus who bore the sufferings of humans. I felt touched; my body felt electrified. I wanted to compose poetry, but not the avant-garde garbage I used to write.

*Liao:* I've been to the church you described—the Sichuan Provincial Catholic Patriotic Church.

*Liu:* At that time, I had no idea that there were government-sanctioned Three-Self patriotic churches and underground house churches. After the service, I went to the local office of the Chinese Patriotic Catholic Association to ask about joining the church. The priest seemed suspicious. Why did I want to become a member of the church? He explained to me the Party's policy on religion and the principles of self-governance, self-support, and self-propagation. He emphasized the need to be patriotic. I asked about the Vatican. He said. "Our Chinese church has nothing to do with the Vatican. They have no control over us." With that, he resumed his lecturing and told me about the application process. "It's good that you want to join the church," he said, "but you have to get a recommendation from your university. Then your application will be reviewed by the church. Then it has to be approved by the local Religious Affairs Bureau. Your file will be kept there." He went on and on. I found it ludicrous. So I interrupted him, "Didn't you just tell me that everyone is equal and we have freedom of religion in this country?" The priest became defensive, "Of course, we have freedom of faith in this country. You just need to go through the proper channels. Why don't you buy a copy of the Bible and read it. Then think it over."

I started reading the Bible he sold me when I got home. It was so disappointing. It was an abridged version, and at the back was an organizational chart putting the Communist Party's Religious Affairs Bureau on top, the Chinese Patriotic Catholic Association beneath it, and then farther down, the Bishops' Conference of the Catholic Church in China, and then bishops, priests, and so forth. It was strange to see that within the church hierarchy, the Communist Party was the big boss. Not God? I went back to the office and asked for a refund. The receptionist said the priest was out and that I should come back later. I was furious and was venting my anger near the entrance to the building, when a woman came up to me and said, "Don't bother trying to get a refund. You should toss it." This was my first meeting with Teacher Bai, my mentor. She lent me her copy of the Bible and said, "If you want to be a true child of the Lord, you should stay away from here. The Chinese Patriotic Catholic Association is satanic."

Teacher Bai led me to her house. Several people were holding a Mass there and it was approaching the end. She introduced me to everyone: "We have a new sister who is suffering. Let's pray for her." About a dozen women recited the Novena Rose Prayer for me. Since then, each time I run into problems in life, I chant the Novena Rose.

*Liao:* Are you still with your mentor?

*Liu:* No. She was arrested soon after I met her. She got seven
   years on charges of conducting illegal religious activities. The
   government has raided many house churches in Chengdu since
   the late 1990s. Several leaders of the underground churches have
   been locked up because they pledged loyalty to the Vatican, not
   the Communist Party. Many underground leaders try to maintain
   contact with the Vatican through secret channels. It's a long story.
   Anyhow, before Teacher Bai was arrested, she introduced me to
   Father Zhang Gangyi, and at Easter in 1993 I went to Zhangerce
   Village in Gaoling County, Shaanxi province, and was baptized
   by Father Zhang. He was eighty-six and his Christian name was
   Anthony. I hope you will always remember this name.

*Liao:* Why's that?

*Liu:* Because he inspired a new generation of Catholics like me. I
   hope to write a book about his life someday.

*Liao:* I only know of Cardinal Gong Pingmei, who was arrested
   in the 1950s for refusing to renounce the Vatican and recognize
   the government-sanctioned church. He was sentenced to thirty
   years. In the late 1970s, while he was still in prison, the pope
   secretly appointed him cardinal and made the appointment public
   in 1991. There was an article in the international section of the
   *People's Daily* about the Foreign Ministry accusing the Vatican of
   meddling in China's internal affairs. The appointment was only
   publicized after the cardinal moved to the United States.

*Liu:* In the past fifty years, many Christians have died because of
   state oppression and persecution. Since the government controls
   the media, we don't hear about most of these martyrs. You
   and other people learned about Cardinal Gong because he was
   singled out by the Party paper as a target for condemnation. That
   was how I heard of Father Zhang. The *People's Daily* carried a

story about him to show how "harmful" religion was to people. "Eliminate superstition and change old customs and traditions," it said. The reporter was very sarcastic. The report went something like this [*Liu recites*]:

A pandemic hit the region lately and many people became sick. Some bad people used the opportunity to spread rumors, saying the pandemic was the result of people's rejection of God. One day, after midnight, locals claimed to have seen a glowing halo on top of what used to be the grave of a foreign missionary. Inside the halo was a figure of Jesus holding a cross. A former Catholic priest immediately gathered a small group of villagers who were backward in their political thinking. He poisoned people's minds with what amounts to demagoguery. He was quoted as saying, "This will be the last time that the Lord will appear to you. God is asking his strayed sheep to return to the right path." This former priest even proclaimed himself to be Jesus's disciple Peter. Moreover, some local people also spread false tales about how this former criminal scooped up water from a stinky ditch near where he stood and then drank it. Within seconds, the ditch turned into a running stream of clean water.

As a result, many sick people heard about the tales and flocked to the spot where the halo had appeared and drank water from the stream of clean water nearby. They were immediately cured and their health had never been better. This myth has deceived the masses, and every day people swarmed to Zhangerce Village, thinking that they had discovered a panacea for their illnesses. When the reporter visited the area for this article, he found that

the dirty ditch was still there and there was no trace of
the clean stream. There was no sign of the holy apparition
there.

At the end of the article, the reporter warned people not to believe in
superstition and admonished them to report to the public health department if there was a pandemic. The reporter also advised people to "be
vigilant against those who spread rumors and report bad people to the
police."

That former priest was Father Zhang Gangyi. I don't know if the
claims of the halo and the clean stream were true or not. They might
have been made up by the Party paper to smear Father Zhang, or maybe
something did happen and the local people have embellished it; you
know how people are. That "negative" story made Father Zhang and
Zhangerce Village famous across the nation. Christians poured in from
all over, some with that very article in their hands. They came to pray
and sought Father Zhang's blessing. Father Zhang helped revive Catholicism in the region. Until he was arrested in late 1989, he held a big
Mass in the local church every Easter.

*Liao:* What have you learned about him?

*Liu:* Father Zhang Gangyi was born in 1907, to a Catholic family
   in Xincheng Village, Xiyang Township. It's in today's Sanyuan
   County, Shaanxi province. At the age of eighteen he joined
   the Tongyuanfang Monastery. Then, he was transferred to a
   monastery in the Ankang diocese in southern Shaanxi province.
   In 1930, he was chosen to join the Franciscan Order, one of
   the best known religious orders within the Catholic Church.
   The Franciscans sponsored his study at its headquarters in
   Rome. He became a novice in 1932 and was ordained a priest on
   August 15, 1937.

When World War II broke out, Pope Pius XII sent Father
Zhang to work as a chaplain at a prisoner-of-war camp in
northern Italy. Thousands of allied soldiers were held there.
Italy under Mussolini was like a big military camp. There were
checkpoints everywhere. According to a popular version of his
story, Father Zhang was arrested and, during interrogation, said
in fluent English, "I'm a priest, not a POW." But his interrogator
didn't agree, "You come from an enemy country and we consider
you a prisoner of war." Father Zhang argued back, "In the eyes
of God, there is no such a thing as an enemy country. There is
only Satan." The interrogator laughed, "In a time of war, our
enemies are Satanic." Father Zhang was held as a prisoner of
war and sent to a camp, probably like those you see in movies
about World War II—barbed wire, spotlights, and guard towers.
Father Zhang spent his time ministering to the allied prisoners,
caring for the wounded, praying for those who needed his
prayers, and led Mass every Sunday. Father Zhang made quite a
name for himself; even Mussolini went to meet him. After that
meeting, Father Zhang was made chaplain for all POW camps
in the region and was relatively free to move around. After Italy
surrendered to the Allied Forces in late 1943, the POW camps
were taken over by the Germans and, in late 1944, Father Zhang
learned that four thousand British and American prisoners were
to be executed. He went to the camp on a rainy night, opened the
gate wide and declared: "You are the children of God. Nobody,
except God, has the right to deprive you of your freedom. Follow
me and leave this hell on earth. Go home and reunite with
your relatives. May God bless you!" The prisoners rushed and
disarmed the guards and successfully escaped.

As to what happened to Father Zhang, there are two versions
of events. The one on the Internet says Father Zhang was

caught by the Nazis and sentenced to death by a military court in Germany. He was supposed to be executed on January 15, 1945, but was rescued in an allied air operation and he spent the remainder of the war in the Vatican. The version I heard in Shaanxi, and for this I can find no corroboration, is amusing. After the prisoners escaped, Father Zhang put on a woman's dress, covered his head with a shawl, and trekked across Italy to Rome and snuck into St. Peter's by a back door. He tailed a priest through the cavernous halls, trying not to get lost, when he lost sight of the priest. As he tried to figure out where to go, he was tripped and fell to floor. It was the priest, who thought he was being followed by a woman. Upon discovering that what he thought was a woman was actually an Asian man in drag, he pulled the shawl off Father Zhang and asked. "Do all oriental men wear head scarves?"

*Liao:* That's certainly a . . . dramatic rendition.

*Liu:* Father Zhang had an audience with the pope. Touched by his story, the pope asked him to continue serving in Vatican City. When the war was over, Father Zhang asked to return to his native China. "The Vatican is merely a city, but its spiritual territory will cover the West and the East," Father Zhang was quoted as saying. "We as missionaries will leave God's footprints around the world."

Before his departure, Father Zhang was awarded a medal by the postwar Italian government for saving the prisoners of war and was invited to say Mass in a cathedral in downtown Rome. At the beginning of 1947, Father Zhang arrived in China. Generalissimo Chiang Kai-shek met with him in Nanjing, the then capital city, and awarded him a "National Hero" medal. He returned to southern Shaanxi province and continued to preach. By the end of 1949, the Chinese civil war was coming to an end and the Nationalist government was on the verge of total collapse. Many of his friends tried to persuade him to leave China, but he chose to stay. "God has chosen me to serve the Chinese people who have been afflicted with catastrophes and sufferings, and to stay here in this chaotic world."

In 1950, Father Zhang was banned from preaching in Ankang. He went home to Sanyuan and, in 1959, was among those who boycotted the government-sanctioned Three-Self patriotic church and maintained their allegiance to the Vatican. He was arrested as a counterrevolutionary spy and sentenced to life imprisonment.

By 1980, as China opened to the West, the government had somewhat relaxed its control over religion and, toward the end of the twenty-first year of his incarceration, Father Zhang was released. When he returned to his native Zhangerce Village, he received letters from the Vatican and the Italian government. The Vatican had been monitoring his situation for two decades. After China and Italy established diplomatic relations, Italian officials attempted to address the issue through diplomatic channels. Neither the Vatican nor the Italian government received a response from Chinese authorities. When Chairman Mao died and the Cultural Revolution was over, a large number of Christians in China had been asked by the Vatican to gather information about Father Zhang and it was learned that he was imprisoned in Shaanxi province. Our new leader, Deng Xiaoping, who had studied abroad when he was young, granted Father Zhang's release. Deng even allowed Father Zhang to make a pilgrimage to the Vatican, which he had not seen in thirty-five years. Rome was packed with tourists and pilgrims, a sharp contrast with the nearly deserted wartime city he remembered.

The buildings were the same, but the people were different. The new pope, John Paul II, was busy and, after waiting for three days, Father Zhang met with a Vatican official, and their conversation went something like this:

The Vatican official greeted him, "On behalf of the pope, we welcome you. We understand that you have suffered tremendously in the past three decades."

Father Zhang remained silent.

The official continued, "Your situation in China should improve fast. We have long known that the Chinese government has set up patriotic church organizations that are independent of the Vatican. You can join the church and offer your service, if you are willing."

Father Zhang asked, "Is this what the new pope wants?"

The official nodded, "Since Deng Xiaoping assumed power, religious activities in communist China have resumed. You should go tend the church of your nation and people under the leadership of the Communist Party."

"Are these also the words of the new pope?" Father Zhang asked.

The Vatican official nodded.

Father Zhang stood up with anger, "Then please go and tell him there is only one center. It is the Vatican. The Vatican is the spiritual capital for Catholics around the world."

Father Zhang's outbursts stunned the official, who stood up and embraced him. "On behalf of the pope, welcome home."

Father Zhang was gripped with emotion when Pope John Paul II received him. He said to Father Zhang during their meeting, "We thought you could have been brainwashed by the Communists. We are glad you haven't changed."

Father Zhang quoted a line from the Bible. "Those who honor me I will honor."

The news of the papal meeting spread quickly and Father Zhang once again became famous in the Catholic communities in China. He had reached an advanced age but his mind remained sharp. After he returned, he went back home, vowing to continue on a path considered as heresy in China. He built a church in his village with money the Italian government had awarded him for his heroic actions during World War II, and built roads for the village. Father Zhang's activities triggered a series of controversies in the region. The local Party featured articles accusing him of spreading superstition. Deng Xiaoping ordered the local government to be tolerant. He didn't want to derail the country's overall reform movement.

*Liao:* In the early to mid—1980s, China experienced a revival of religion.

*Liu:* Yes, Catholicism, previously considered "the spiritual opium of foreign imperialists," was allowed to expand. Catholic preachers could practice in the open. In 1980 about three hundred Catholic leaders in China met in Shanghai, the first such meeting after the Cultural Revolution. The Vatican requested through diplomatic channels that a papal envoy be allowed to attend. The Chinese government rejected the request. Because the Catholic Church was under the jurisdiction of the Religious Affairs Bureau, the premise for any type of religious freedom was patriotism. Father Zhang was outraged and asked government officials to reconsider the Vatican's request. "The pope in the Vatican is the physical and spiritual leader of Catholics in the world, including Catholics in every diocese in China. He embodies the supreme power of Jesus Christ, and no secular government is in the position to change it with any secular excuses."

Because of his stand, Father Zhang became the target of condemnation by the church leaders. Several priests and bishops rebuked him, accusing him of being a traitor to his own country and leading the Chinese Catholics on a dangerous path. It was like a Mao-era public denunciation.

Father Zhang quoted Paul's letter to Timothy from the Bible: "[Jesus] appeared in a body, was vindicated by the Spirit, was seen by angels, was preached among the nations, was believed by the world, was taken up in glory." He then asked, "Do you think officials at the Religious Affairs Bureau understand the meaning of these words? They, including many of you, probably haven't read the Bible. Do you know that revising the Lord's words is considered a cardinal and unforgivable sin?"

Considering Father Zhang's prominent international status, the chair didn't kick him out of the meeting. Instead, he put Father Zhang's request to a vote, to show the "democratic" nature of the leading body. When the meeting was asked for a show of hands on whether the pope is the only spiritual leader of Catholics in China, there was total silence—with one lone hand raised, that of Father Zhang. He kept his arm raised throughout the four-hour meeting as the other 351 clerics ignored him.

*Liao:* What happened later?

*Liu:* Father Zhang walked out of the church, still with his hand raised. It was already dark and the streets were crowded. He looked up to the sky, shouted "Lord!" and then collapsed on the stairs. He was taken to a hospital.

After the government crackdown at Tiananmen Square in June 1989, Father Zhang openly condemned the use of force. At Mass, he prayed for the dead and wounded. On November 21, a group of bishops and priests who refused to join government churches gathered in Zhangerce Village. They formed the Chinese

Mainland Catholic Bishops Conference. Bishop Fan Xueyan of the Baoding diocese was elected chair. The organization was meant to counter the influence of the progovernment Bishops' Conference of the Catholic Church in China. Barely two weeks later, Father Zhang was detained by local police for interrogation. They held him until June 12, 1990. Father Zhang continued his fight for the church's independence from the state until his death in 1997. He was ninety.

*Liao:* What did he inspire in you as a Catholic? Are you willing to follow in his footsteps and preach, despite the dangers ahead for you?

*Liu:* I try. I traveled to the rural areas, visited coal mines—one time, I preached the gospel underground, in total darkness—and prayed in cemeteries for children who had died of mistreatment. I have been chased by police many times, and I've been in and out of prison several times. The longest jail sentence was eight months. I was forbidden to pray, and each time I did so, they would beat me. They designed all sorts of ways to torture me. My will has weakened. I'm scared to death. I don't want to die in China. I want to leave.

*Liao:* Any luck so far?

*Liu:* I lock my door and stay home to pray. I do the Novena Rose three times a day. I hope I can overcome my fear and reach a country favored by God.

*Chapter 16*


## THE BLIND MUSICIAN


Wen Huachun is a blind street musician in Chengdu. He lives on the second floor of a run-down building in a sparsely furnished apartment; there's a table, four benches, an old television, and an array of musical instruments Wen says he had made himself. Wen is an accomplished player of the two-stringed erhu. On the wall next to the window is a large poster of the Beatles.

A poet friend, Jiang Ji, had heard about my project and, on March 25, 2006, took me to meet Wen. I'd seen him perform, singing and playing the erhu while pedaling a homemade organ, in the Baiguolin district where I live, and I even had tossed him two yuan one day when he sang "Stepping into a New Era." There's a line I particularly like: "The new leadership carry forward the cause of our pioneers and lead us into a new era . . ."

We were met at the entrance to the building by Wen's wife, twenty years younger than he. She comes from a rural village. Her pretty face exuded warmth and determination. She said she was attracted to his talent and strong personality and knew she would spend the rest of her life with him. After their marriage, she bought a flatbed tricycle with which she pedals her husband and his musical equipment around the city. "I'm his wife, chauffeur, nanny, bodyguard, and eyes," she joked. Wen must have heard our talking in the hallway and opened the door. I recognized that smiley face right away.

I told him about hearing him perform "Stepping into a New Era" and mentioned it seemed to be popular among blind street musicians: I'd heard it performed in Urumqi in the far northwest and in Beijing, but I liked his version best because he used blaring amplifiers. Wen said with mock aggression, "Are you making fun of us?" I laughed, "Would I dare?"

*Wen Huachun:* You know, times have changed and society is moving
    forward. We have to watch our backs and be optimistic about
    the future. Coping with the Communist Party is like handling a
    big tiger. You can pat and brush it, but you must be gentle. If you
    brush in the wrong direction, you'll be in big trouble. I think this
    applies to both the blind and normal people. We have to "step into
    a new era."
*Liao Yiwu:* Tell me about your life. How did you lose your sight?
*Wen:* I was born on December 8, 1944, in Huangjiaoye, on the
    south side of Chongqing city. As an infant, according to my
    mom, I had perfect eyesight. Everyone liked me because I never
    cried. I remember my mother taking me to wedding banquets
    and people around the table treating me like a dish, passing me
    around and smacking their lips to tease me. The hosts would
    always fill my pockets with candies. I also remember chasing
    and catching chickens in the yard. Even now, I can still see in my
    mind the old streets and the stores near my house. My grandma
    used to carry me on her back. She bought me tofu soup from
    street vendors. Then, in September 1947, before I turned three,
    my nanny realized I had what the locals called "rooster eyes."
*Liao:* What's that?
*Wen:* I could see fine in daylight, but at night, nothing. I was like
    a rooster. It was like my eyes were covered with a heavy curtain
    that couldn't be lifted. I don't know if you notice, when a rooster

looks at something on the ground, it tilts its head. When I was going blind, I would do the same, tilting my head and trying to see. Sometimes, my neck would crane forward. Eventually, I couldn't see anything at all and would cry and rub my eyes.

*Liao:* Was it some kind of infection?

*Wen:* I don't know. My parents were busy with their business in the city. I was raised in the countryside by a nanny. In those days, children were not treated like they are today. My nanny had several children of her own. She had to farm in the field during the day and do house chores at night. She breast-fed me during breaks. So I spent most of my days crawling around on the floor, my face covered with dirt and mud.

But you know how people in Chongqing love spicy food! I started eating spicy food at a very young age, before I could even walk steadily. I would carry a big bowl of rice topped with a thick layer of red peppers. They were so hot that sweat and snot and tears streamed down my face. It was so good. People who didn't know me would have thought that I was being punished for some misdeed. On summer days, I would sit around a hot pot and dip raw meat in hot spicy broth. My clothes were soaked with sweat. I would strip down to my underwear. When my parents moved me back to the city, they had to take a whole jar of peppers away from me because I broke out in a rash all over, on the corners of my mouth, inside my armpits, and on my back. There were two big red sores on each side of my temple, as big as peanuts. I kept scratching them, and they became infected. They had to take me to see a doctor. Seeing how painful it was, they forbade me from eating spicy food. I refused to eat and would smash my bowl in protest. So maybe it was too much hot food that caused my blindness.

My nanny came to see me one day, and when I heard her

talking in the courtyard, I rushed out of the house, but I was groping my way and tripped and hurt my head. She clutched me to her bosom, examined my eyes in the sun, and said, "It's terrible. The child has rooster eyes." The nanny also told my grandma that she had taken me to a fortune-teller once and the master had said disability would be part of my fate.

So I was probably destined to be blind. But, according to my nanny, the master also saw another possible future as he did his calculations based on the hour, date, and year of my birth. "This child could be a powerful figure, a government official, at least at the county level. But you have to keep him in the countryside until he is three years old. Otherwise, his fate could change. He could end up with a disability either on the face or on his feet." Unfortunately, my parents brought me back to the city three months before my third birthday.

*Liao:* Do you believe such things?

*Wen:* I do. My grandma took me to another fortune-teller when I turned four. That person said similar things about my future.

*Liao:* What did the doctors say about your sight?

*Wen:* I used to have a sister, a year older. She died of smallpox in 1946. Since I was then their only child, my parents really doted on me. They took me to hospitals and spent lots of money on eye specialists. My mother had to pawn almost everything to cover the medical expenses. All the doctors gave the same diagnosis— the nerves in my eyes were damaged. I had tried all sorts of meds—herbs, pills, ointments, injections. I probably saw more than twenty doctors in the space of a year. My parents became discouraged. The family was broke and I was still blind. At that desperate moment, someone recommended we see a foreign doctor, a missionary.

The friend said the foreigner was a priest and worked for a

church hospital on the top of Wang Mountain. He claimed to be doing God's work. My father was a little skeptical. Would the foreigner treat a nonbeliever? That friend, who was a follower of that foreign religion, reassured my father that God treated every sufferer equally. So we went. The friend took us to the hospital.

*Liao:* It must have been a Catholic hospital.

*Wen:* I have no idea. In my neighborhood, people call Christianity "yang-jiao" or "the foreign religion." It was quite popular. The Nationalist government had temporarily moved its capital from Nanjing to Chongqing during the Japanese invasion. Many Americans ended up living in my city. Plus, Generalissimo Chiang Kai-shek and his wife were both Christians. Before and after World War II, many Western missionaries came to Chongqing. They built several churches, hospitals, and charity centers. Our indigenous Buddhist and Taoist religions only require people to burn incense and worship.

*Liao:* Where was Wang Mountain?

*Wen:* It wasn't far from my home in Huangjiaoya, next to Huangshan in Chongqing, where Chiang Kai-shek used to stay. My parents left in the morning and didn't come back until late in the afternoon. They brought back a bottle of eye drops. I was playing by the entrance. They told me excitedly: "Baby, sit still. We're going to wash your eyes." I sat still. I was tired of being in the dark. For people born with blindness, the darkness is all they know, but I used to be able to see and it was hard for me then.

Before they used the eye drops, I was washed with a wet cloth—Grandma used up two basins of water—and the area around my eyes was cleaned and sterilized with alcohol-soaked cotton balls my parents brought back from the hospital. The missionary doctor must have told them to do all that. After about a week, I could tell the difference between light and dark, and after a few months I could tell when the sun was setting. It was like light splashing all over me. And I could make out people as shadows and could point at trees. Everyone was crying with excitement, and neighbors rushed over to find out the cause of the commotion. Someone said, "This child is truly blessed. God has performed a miracle."

My parents felt very encouraged by the improvement and, as the daily treatment continued, the fog began to dissipate. My grandma prepared a gift so my parents could give it to the doctor.

*Liao:* What was in the eye drops?

*Wen:* I have no idea.

*Liao:* Didn't your parents tell you the name of the medicine?

*Wen:* I don't think my parents knew either.

*Liao:* How much did your parents pay?

*Wen:* Not a penny. The doctor said he was doing God's work.

My eyesight was improving bit by bit as I turned five. Communist troops were approaching the city. We could hear gunfire and booming cannons day and night. There were Nationalist troops in the city. It took the Communists a long time to crush their defenses. Stray bullets would fly over our roof like locusts, smashing many tiles. No one moved around outside.

When the bottle of eye drops was empty, and despite the chaos and dangers, my parents insisted on going to get more. They left early in the morning and were back before dusk, exhausted, distraught. With the Nationalist government about to be defeated, all the foreigners in Chongqing, even the missionaries, had evacuated. By the time my parents got to the hospital, it was deserted. Shooting continued for another three days and then, quite abruptly, stopped. My grandma said the Communist troops had taken the city. There were fireworks. People were dancing and singing. Chongqing was "liberated."

It was all fate. The founding of the new Communist China robbed me of my sight, but I knew never to say so in public. For the next few years, I could still see light and could see people from their shadows, but gradually I was back in darkness. My parents kept trying to find the cure the foreign doctor had held out to them. Each time they took me to a new Chinese doctor, all he or she would say was that it was too late. My eyeballs were shrinking. If you look at me now, my eye sockets appear to be empty.

In the end, they gave up and heeded the master's other warning, that I should learn a skill so I could support myself. I was quite smart back then and quite likeable. It turned out I was good with music, and I liked it, so it was decided I should become a blind musician.

The street in front of my house was called Artist Street. Many street musicians and performers—dancers, acrobats, violinists, erhu players, and flautists—liked to gather there. I followed the musicians around and picked up some skills. A next-door neighbor, whom I called Uncle Yuan, taught me how to play the flute. Not long after that, I took erhu lessons from Mr. Li, a blind person who lived down the street. Soon I could perform myself. I was far from being a first-class erhu player or flautist, but I could play some tunes fairly well.

We had to do lots of revolutionary tunes to drum up support for the various national and local political campaigns, such as the war against the Americans in Korea, the Three-Anti movement, campaigns to prevent fire and theft and expose imperialist spies, the Sino-Soviet alliance, the Anti-Rightist campaign, and the

Great Leap Forward. We had to do lots of songs, but I learned
them very fast. I only needed to rehearse a couple of times and I
had them memorized.

There used to be a song to warn people against imperialist
spies: "When it is dark, you need to lock the door. If a stranger
knocks, you need to ask, you need to think before you talk. You
need to open your eyes and perk up your ears because he might
be collecting intelligence." Other songs encouraged people to
rally against the counterrevolutionaries and Rightists.

The street committee assigned me to be an erhu player in a
small orchestra. I had memorized a thousand tunes and earned
several awards. During the famine, people were starving, but
the government still sent us out to perform. I was quite young.
I didn't get a salary but earned a lot of coupons, which could be
exchanged for food, but that only worked when there was food to
be had. My family starved several times.

*Liao:* What did you perform in the years of the famine?

*Wen:* The same old upbeat revolutionary songs, praising the great
leadership of the Party and singing about the wonderful life we
had. Since I worked really hard, I continued to win awards. At
public meetings for disabled people, the street-committee chair
would call me to the podium and hand me a red certificate. After
the meeting, I could exchange the certificate for a bowl of sweet
potatoes. Our performance troupe was disbanded during the
Cultural Revolution because so many revolutionary singing and
dance troupes were formed. They no longer needed disabled
people to perform. So I became unemployed.

*Liao:* Were you affected in other ways by the Cultural Revolution?

*Wen:* No, at least not at the beginning. I just stayed home, without
anything to do. At the tail end of the Cultural Revolution, since
everyone was fed up with the limited entertainment choices,

some young people started to hang out with me. I taught them to play the erhu, and it got so my house was packed all the time. I would teach them old songs from the 1950s, even some love songs from pre-Communist days. I accompanied their singing with my erhu or flute. Occasionally, I would dig out some old LPs from the attic and play them on an old gramophone. We would also listen to shortwave radio and hear music programs from overseas; we had to be very careful because anyone caught listening to shortwave radio was sent to prison. But young people like taking risks, so we had a lot of fun. Soon, however, the street committee got wind of it and reported me to the police, accusing me of running an "underground club." Police came one night and searched my place. They took me away for interrogation. They found nothing and I was released. Over the next few years, they would search my place in the middle of the night. I was in and out of the detention center. But since I was a blind person, they found it hard to imprison me.

Chairman Mao finally died. The Cultural Revolution ended. I had to go make a living. I tried performing on the street and discovered that people liked my music; I made enough to get by. The police harassed me now and then. They would confiscate my musical instruments or detain me for a few days. As soon as they released me, I was back on the street again. I think they just didn't know what to do about me.

It's been thirty some years since I started my street-musician career. I'm a veteran now. I moved to Chengdu several years ago. The media have written many positive stories about me. But the police still watch me closely, detaining me and levying fines on me. I'm used to it.

*Liao:* Why do you have a poster of the Beatles on your wall?

*Wen:* I love their songs. Someday, I hope to travel abroad and perform on the streets in America. And when I'm there, I want to find out what kind of eye drops that American missionary gave me. It's been bugging me for years and years.

*Liao:* Still, if you hadn't lost your sight, you would not have been the brilliant street musician you are.


## Epilogue

What was in the missionary doctor's eye drops that almost saved Wen Huachun's sight? I consulted with Liu Shahe, a well-known historian in Chengdu.

"Fish oil," he said. "It's a commonplace supplement by today's standards. But for mountain people, fish was rarely on the menu, and fish oil, which helps the body absorb nutrients, was unheard of. Who would have thought that the eyes needed feeding, just like the mouth? Well, Western doctors figured this out, extracted fish oil, and made it into eye drops." According to Liu, eye drops made from fish oil helped lots of blind people in China before the Communist revolution.

*Chapter 17*

## THE ORPHANAGE

I was born under Communism in China and was educated by that system—certain things were "true" and should be accepted, never questioned. And in Mao's China, religion was "evil" and those who believed in religion were at best deluded and in need of re-education, at worst cultists or imperialist spies whose aim was to undermine the country. I was brought up believing that Christian orphanages and Christian hospitals were among the scariest places on earth.

In elementary school, my teacher said that foreign missionaries came to China to enslave and murder the Chinese people. The nuns who ran orphanages were monsters, we learned, and though I later came to comprehend the humorous stereotype of the disciplinarian nun among Catholics around the world, in China, they assumed nightmarish characteristics. Children taken in from poor families were raised in pots, and when they reached their teenage years, the nuns would break the pots and let them out. By then, they had become pygmies and would be forced to sit on a table all day and pray to their "God." The pygmies were never allowed to run around.

In the course of my research, I came across an old news story issued by the state-run news agency, Xinhua, on June 5, 1964, and written by a journalist named Zhong Yuwen. It usefully illustrates how Christian missionary work was used in cultivating a wider hostility toward the West:

## THE WORLD HAS CHANGED

### Visiting a Children's Hospital in Nanjing
### June 5, 1964

On International Children's Day of June 1, many young elementary school teachers and students came to visit the Nanjing Municipal Children's Hospital. Upon their request, a doctor shared with the young visitors the hospital's history.

In the 1940s, after ruthlessly exploiting and brutally oppressing its people for many years, the Nationalist government and other reactionaries initiated a civil war, plunging the country into chaos and bringing more hardship to its people. Many families had been ruined. Thousands of innocent children became orphaned. At that time, at the instigation of foreign imperialists, a group of foreign nuns, cloaked in religion, arrived in the city. Their ultimate goal was to service the counterrevolutionaries. They put on a so-called benevolent face of charity to win over people. They built a house near Guangzhou Road and started a "Sacred Heart Children's Home," adopting abandoned children. They abused the children and turned the Sacred Heart Children's Home into a hell on earth and a children's death camp. They ruthlessly reduced children's food ration, adding a little milk to half a pound of thin rice and pea powder gruel every day. For a one-year-old, they only fed them rice gruel four times a day. For three or four year olds, they fed the same thin rice gruel three times daily. As a consequence, children suffered from malnutrition. They looked thin as dry wood sticks. Osteoporosis was prevalent. Many three-year-olds had problems straightening their backs; some four-year-olds still couldn't walk. Many three-year-olds only weighed five to six kilograms. The nuns never took good care of the children and most of them had been afflicted with eczema and bed sores. Crying was supposed to be a child's instinctive behavior but many children didn't even have the strength to cry. They lay there silently, waiting to die. The mortality rate there was over 70 percent. When children died, those so-called philanthropists would murmur the following line with delight: "We should be happy for their deaths because their souls will land in heaven."

In addition to abusing children physically, the nuns also poisoned their minds. Every morning, older children were forced to kneel on the cold cement floor of the church and pray, asking for God to forgive their sins. They constantly invoked God to intimidate children, asking them to beg God for forgiveness. As a consequence, children lived in constant fear and had very low self-esteem. The nuns also gave the children English names, such as Maria, Andrew, Philip, and Matilda, imposing foreign education on them so they would remain ignorant of their own motherland. In this way, the children could easily be enslaved by the imperialists.

After the Communists came and liberated the city, those children were rescued. Acting on the demands of the great masses, the people's government punished the foreign imperialists according to law and took over the Sacred Heart Children's Home, providing medical care to the children. Under the care of the Communist Party, the children grew up healthily, like seedlings in drought being showered with blissful rainfall. In 1953, the government converted the place where Chinese children were abused by foreign imperialists into a children's hospital. Under the care and encouragement of the Communist Party, doctors and nurses have contributed their share to the cause of protecting the health of Chinese children.

I shared this story with my historian friend, the seventy-five-year-old Liu Shahe, who lives next to the Benevolence Temple in downtown Chengdu. He said that the Communist government was not the first to concoct lies and stir up hatred against Christian missionaries:

*Liu Shahe:* As a child, I used to hear that Catholic nuns were vampires who sucked blood from poor Chinese children and plucked out their eyeballs to use as decorations. People began to spread unfounded rumors way before the Boxer Rebellion, an anti-Christian movement in Northern China from 1898 to 1901. There was a notorious incident in Sichuan province. In 1896, a Christian hospital, which is now the Chengdu No. 2 Municipal People's Hospital, was mobbed by local residents who claimed doctors had lured gullible children into the hospital with candies, then killed them, soaked their bodies in pickle jars, and ate their flesh. Several hundred angry residents smashed the windows and took over the hospital. All the doctors and nurses fled and some hid inside a church on Shaanxi Road. Residents eventually attacked the church and set it on fire. In the end, it turned out that one resident had passed the hospital lab and saw tissue samples of a dead baby stored in formaldehyde. The story took on a life of its own as it spread among the public.

*Liao Yiwu:* Hostility against missionaries continued under Communist rule.

*Liu:* The government propaganda machine perpetuated those rumors and spread new lies to stoke hatred against Christians and force people to relinquish their religions. The Xinhua report you showed me was a perfect example.

In the pre-Communist days, especially around World War II, many Americans, including diplomats, military personnel, and missionaries, came to Chongqing and Chengdu. They built airports, hospitals, and many orphanages. In the spring of 1945, Chengdu was hit by a cholera epidemic. Bodies littered the streets. All the coffins were sold out, and hospitals were packed with dying patients. A French Christian hospital on Ping'anqiao Street opened its doors to the public, and patients swarmed in. When all the beds had been taken, patients crowded the hallways and spilled over into the courtyard. French doctors and nurses worked day and night. When they ran out of drugs, they administered oral and IV rehydration solutions. Sometimes, when patients were brought in, it was already too late. The Christian doctors and nurses still wouldn't give up and tried their best to save lives.

I used to know an American nun. Since her first name started with *M*, which sounded like the Chinese word "Mann," we all called her Sister Mann. She had lived in Chengdu for many years and offered free training and workshops for young women who wanted to be midwives. As you know, in the old days women growing up in wealthy families didn't want to take midwifery as a career, whereas those from poor families might want to do the job but didn't have money to attend midwifery school. As a consequence, the infant mortality rate in Sichuan province was high. Of course, the Nationalist government also engaged in similar projects, but I think Sister Mann's contributions were more prominent. She belonged to an American Christian mission hospital here. This Sister Mann was also a writer and published several books. You probably have heard about writer Han Suyin [*Love Is a Many-Splendored Thing*], who maintained close relations with the first generation of Chinese Communist leaders. In the late 1930s, Han Suyin worked at the same hospital as Sister Mann. The two became good friends. Han practiced her writing on Sister Mann's typewriter. After the Communist takeover in

1949, Han Suyin went to practice medicine in Southeast Asia, but Sister Mann stayed in Chengdu and continued running her workshop. She saw Chengdu as her permanent home. In the early 1950s, the government required all schools to hang portraits of Chairman Mao in classrooms. As a Christian, Sister Mann rejected the government demands. The local leaders came to talk with her, to persuade her to comply. She wouldn't budge. One day, while Sister Mann was away, the leaders pasted a poster of Mao on the wall above the blackboard. When she came back, she noticed the poster and was outraged. She found a ladder, climbed up, and ripped the poster off. That greatly offended the authorities. Local leaders openly accused her of being an imperialist spy and kicked her out of the country.

Sister Mann returned to the United States, and Han Suyin went to visit her in the 1960s. Han found out that Sister Mann had no interest in politics. She never badmouthed the Communist Party. She didn't rip down Mao's poster for political reasons; she simply believed the secular government should not place its authority above that of God.

*Liao:* Was this attitude prevalent?

*Liu:* Sister Mann's story is not unique. When the Communist government rose to power, they rewrote history and portrayed Western Christian missionaries as monsters and saboteurs. Many missionaries who had worked and lived in China for decades were forced out of the country. All their charity work was used as evidence against Western countries, which the government claimed attempted to colonize and enslave the Chinese people. Christianity is thriving again in China. It is the job of historians and writers to uncover the historical truth and explain it to the public.

# Chapter 18

## THE NEW CONVERT

Shangshuyuan used to be home to a Catholic seminary, the Seminarium Annuntiationis, construction of which was begun by Bishop Marie-Hulien Dunand, a French missionary of the Chengdu diocese, in 1895. It took thirteen years to complete, a vast building in the gothic style covering eighteen thousand square meters that turned out a generation of priests to serve southwest China. A century later, it was a crumbling edifice. The excesses of the Cultural Revolution helped hasten what wind and rain were already doing. When I first visited in early 2000, it stood naked and lonely and skeletal.

In May 2008, as two newlyweds, the groom in a black suit and the bride in a Western-style white wedding gown, posed for portraits in front of the site, the earth began to shake and the remaining structures of the chapel collapsed around them. Within seconds, what had been left of the Seminarium Annuntiationis was gone. Pictures spread quickly on the Internet. The 2008 Sichuan earthquake claimed the lives of nearly seventy thousand people. It was a powerful quake, more powerful than even the Red Guard.

On the afternoon of January 13, 2010, while having tea with my sister in Bailu Township at Shangshuyuan, I overheard a group of fashionably dressed young men talking about the Sichuan earthquake and was drawn into their conversation. It emerged that one of their number,

Ho Lu, who was twenty-four, had recently become a Christian, and when he admitted that the quake "still creeps me out" and suggested we change the subject, I asked if he would talk about what led him to Christianity.

*Ho Lu:* I started going to church with my mother when I was a child. Then, when I was in high school, I was quite a rebel. I hated everything my parents did to me, and I gave up on the church. But over the past two years, I think I have been getting more mature and decided to go back to church. I was baptized six months ago.

*Liao Yiwu:* So, you came full circle.

*Ho:* I guess. I figure we probably have to run many circles in life, but the more circles we run in, the more confused we become. Look at those old ladies in the park. Every morning and evening, they hang out, do weird dances, practice tai chi and do aerobics, and sing their hearts out to some Chinese operatic tunes. They swing their butts and do all sorts of weird stuff. I sometimes wonder why they bother. Do they want to get rid of the fat around their fleshy tummies? Do they hope to live forever?

*Liao:* Hey, hey, be nice. They could be your parents, or grandparents.

*Ho:* Whatever. My dad is a Buddhist, and my mom believes in Jesus. My grandpa teaches ancient Chinese literature at the University of Sichuan. Each time I visit, he's swaying his head and reciting some ancient prose or poems; he loves Taoist philosophy and constantly blabbers to me lines from Zhuangzi, the Taoist master. "In the northern darkness there is a fish and his name is Kun. The Kun is so huge I don't know how many thousand li he measures. He changes and becomes a bird whose name is Peng. The back of the Peng measures I don't know how many thousand li across . . . blah, blah, blah."

Anyhow, three religions are practiced in our home. Everyone does his or her own stuff. Why can't they form a uniform family religion so we don't have to fight all the time? It's kind of strange. As a kid, I would go with my dad to Buddhist temples and mimic the gestures and facial expressions of the Buddhist statues. I would sit cross-legged in lotus positions, with my eyes closed. I made adults laugh so hard. When I was with my mom, I would attend services at an old church. People sang hymns. It was kind of grand and cool.

I prefer Christianity. Buddhism is too regional, secular, and not cool. Those old men and women, those wealthy businessmen or government officials, go to the temples, burning incense and praying for trivial stuff, such as more money, more promotions, and more luck. Taoism is way too highbrow, not attainable. I think Christianity is the only one that's all encompassing. Jesus was crucified, and his blood redeemed us of our sins. Imagine how painful it was for him, but he did it for the salvation of humanity.

My parents filed for divorce a few years ago. I remember they used to argue about religion all the time. My mom wanted my dad to give up Buddhism and turn to Christianity. My dad totally ignored her. My mom would ask my dad to give some serious thought to Christianity. My dad would shoot back by saying, "I don't need to think further. Buddhism is suitable for Chinese like me." My mom wouldn't cave in. She would go, "Buddhism came here from India. Look at what Buddhism has done to the two big poor and backward countries." My dad would go: "Okay, please go ahead and use your Christian faith to make China a wealthy and advanced country. I'm happy where I am, backward and poor." My mom would end up shaking her head and saying: "It's so degrading to live with a pagan under the same roof."

*Liao:* When did your mom become a Christian?

*Ho:* When she was pregnant with me.

*Liao:* In 1985? That was a few years after the government relaxed its control over religion.

*Ho:* My mom found God quite by chance. An old friend introduced her to a Protestant church nearby. She went there a couple of times for Sunday services. She felt inspired. A seventy-year-old minister baptized her. Many people were there to watch. My mother was a high school teacher. She teaches Chinese. In those days, it was a big deal for a high school teacher to be converted. Many people didn't approve.

*Liao:* Sounds like your mother belongs to a Three-Self church.

*Ho:* Yes. I saw a sign posted on the entrance. It states the church is part of the Chinese Christian Three-Self Patriotic Movement. Mom's church is quite old, with over one hundred years of history. The minister started serving in the church way before the Communists came. He just passed away. You should see the inside, very cool, old with traditional decor.

*Liao:* I assume the church must have reviewed her history and political background. The government indirectly controls the recruitment process.

*Ho:* I don't know whether they did or not. I do know that the church was real cautious with new members. I heard that my mom's boss at school tried to talk her out of it, but she was quite persistent. In the end, the school authorities okayed her request and set some parameters for her: mainly, she was not allowed to talk about Christianity to her students in class. When I was growing up, my mom used to say I was half converted because I was inside her womb when she was baptized.

*Liao:* Do you know any members from an underground church?

*Ho:* No. When my mom joined the church in 1985, there was no underground church in Chengdu . . . I don't think it's a big deal. We only have one God, who leads us all. It doesn't matter where you worship.

*Liao:* Have you heard of Reverend Wu Yaozong?

*Ho:* The name sounds familiar. I don't know to which dynasties he belonged.

*Liao:* He was one of the people who founded China's Three-Self Patriot Movement in the early 1950s. They proposed that the Chinese Christian churches should sever their ties with the Western imperialists and engage in self-governance, self-support, and self-propagation. Many Christians didn't agree with him. They don't believe churches should be under the rule of the Chinese government.

*Ho:* I agree. I think Wu Yaozong's idea was so crazy and insane. The Lord Jesus comes from the West. Christianity is predominantly a Western religion. How could you cut yourself off from the West?

*Liao:* That's an interesting point. What prompted you to be baptized?

*Ho:* It's a long story. My mom used to bug me about my schoolwork all the time. She also sent me to study painting. I think she hoped I would be ranked at the top of my class. When I was little, I was too weak to fight her; I accepted everything she sent my way. After I grew up, I no longer obeyed her. During my last year in high school, I refused to take part in the national college examinations. My mom had a fit. She cried and prayed every

day, asking God to give her more confidence and power. To
tell you the truth, I was suffering from examination phobia. I
couldn't concentrate on my classes. I used to have four classes in
the morning. By the time I was in my fourth class, I started to be
seized with the urge to scream. I wanted to smash the desks and
chairs. So I told my mom about it. She took me to see a doctor,
who diagnosed me as suffering from "intermittent anxiety."
Seeing that I wasn't too far away from being a lunatic, she let me
alone and stopped pressuring me. She also encouraged me to play
and to surf the Internet. I did a lot of that. I was very into pop
stars, especially Chinese rock stars.

*Liao:* Tell me, did you date in high school?

*Ho:* Dating? You hick! We started dating back in elementary school.
I tasted my "forbidden fruits" at the age of fourteen. By the time
I was in senior high school, I was a veteran. What choices do we
have? The food we eat contains too many hormones; our bodies
mature fast.

*Liao:* Interesting. Sorry for the digression. What happened later?

*Ho:* I didn't attend college. I couldn't find a job to support myself
either. I just idled at home all day. When the Hunan TV station
ran the *Chinese Idol* show, I didn't miss a single episode. I loved all
the female contestants, especially Li Yuchun. She's avant-garde
and sexy. She's super cool. Each time she came on, I was always
excited, jumping up and down.

*Liao:* Li Yuchun? The singer who looks androgynous? I can't
understand a word she sings.

*Ho:* You sound like my mom. That's exactly what she said. But
really, it's pointless to argue over the trivial stuff. Now that
I'm a Christian, I have become more serious about life. I feel
embarrassed by my wild teenage behavior. You know, when I was
in high school, my mother would encourage me to read the Bible.

Instead of studying it, I tried giving her a hard time by finding faults in it. And that was pretty easy. For example, in Genesis, we are told that God created Adam and Eve and allowed them to live without worries in Eden and have anything they wanted, but not the fruit that would allow them to know good from evil. Adam and Eve couldn't resist the temptation put before them by Satan, and they ate the forbidden fruit. This outraged God, and they were driven out of Eden. So, humans started their long history as exiles. After reading that, I believed that God was like the Chinese government, trying to rule humans with a policy to keep them in ignorance. I made my mom really mad.

*Liao:* At least you read things with a critical mind.

*Ho:* Glad you think that way. Anyhow, I idled around the house for two years and constantly got into fights with my mom. Since I passed the college age, going to school was no longer an option. Watching *Chinese Idol* couldn't be counted as a profession. So I told her I would go look for a job. But it was hard. I didn't have any talents or skills. Besides, I had stayed home for too long. My limbs had become weak. Even a little bit of physical labor made my heart beat fast and muscles ache. Then my dad got me a job through a friend. I was supposed to work as a company security guard. The first day on the job, I carried my MP4 player. One day my boss tried to talk to me, but I couldn't hear him because I had the headset on. I just kept walking, enjoying Li Yuchun's songs. When my boss caught up with me, he grabbed me by the shoulder and howled in his thunderous voice: "Get out of here. You're fired."

My parents got really sick of me. They were too tired to even scold me. My mom and dad met to figure out what to do about me. My dad kept shaking his head, saying, "I don't know when he will grow up. Let's put a hold on finding him any jobs. Let

him stay home until he's twenty-five. Maybe by then he will
be mature enough to handle a job." My mom had to agree. She
consoled herself by saying, "There are so many young people
staying home nowadays. At least, he's not alone."

*Liao:* How could you take it?

*Ho:* I couldn't have cared less. I was in no hurry. I didn't have a
girlfriend to pester me. My mom cooked for me and bought me
clothes. I got pocket money each month. It wasn't bad. But one
day, I became bored at home. I opened up the Bible and flipped
the pages and stopped at a passage in the book of Jeremiah: "'If
you will return, O Israel, return to me,' declares the LORD. 'If
you put your detestable idols out of my sight and no longer go
astray, and if in a truthful, just and righteous way you swear, as
surely as the LORD lives, then the nations will be blessed by him
and in him they will glory.'"

I was totally, like, thunderstruck. My mind blanked out for a
few minutes. My God, I thought about all those detestable pop
idols that I had worshipped—Li Yuchun and Jay Chou. They
ran past my mind like floating clouds. The Lord knew me well.
He understood my generation well. We had been plunged into a
bottomless pit of pop icon worshipping. I couldn't get myself out,
and my life had almost been ruined. God finally revealed himself
to me. His words were stern. I had to remove all the idols out of
his sight, and I swore to be good.

When my mother came home that night, I told her that I
wanted to be a Christian and I wanted to be baptized. She looked
bewildered and didn't know what to say.

*Liao:* That was quite a sudden change.

*Ho:* If you really believe in God, you should be baptized. If you
don't, suit yourself. That was what I thought at that time. I'm a
prototype of the posteighties generation. For years, I followed all

sorts of pop icons and knew how to sing all their songs. When a
new one came along, I discarded the old ones. I spent my whole
life chasing idols like a dog chasing a ball. But then I learned to
sing hymns and I never get tired of them. The hymns touch me
on a deeper level. They change me. We used to have very free
discussions at the church. When I confessed to my Christian
brothers and sisters about my problems and my doubts about life,
no one laughed at me or thought I was stupid. When I told them I
didn't have a job, they all helped me. I got several interviews with
different companies. During each interview, I would say: "I'm
a Christian; I'm young and inexperienced, but I'm hardworking
and dedicated. If you don't want to offer the job to me, offer me
an internship or I can volunteer. If you decide that I'm really
good, hire me or pay me later."

*Liao:* Did you get a job?

*Ho:* Yep. I do web maintenance for a company right now.

*Liao:* Have you attended services at someone's house?

*Ho:* A couple of times. I know some Christians who even gather
and worship inside office buildings. But it doesn't feel right.
Worshipping inside a church makes me feel good. I guess my
generation just likes beautiful things.

*Liao:* You guys pay attention to superficial stuff, the packaging, not
the content.

*Ho:* What's wrong with that? Since ancient times, humans have
always been attracted to beautiful things. We first wrapped
ourselves with animal skin. Then we began to wear clothes. It's
all about packaging ourselves and looking nice. When we face
the Lord, we need to look clean and decent. When the Lord is in
heaven, he also keeps the palace clean and neat so he can be in the
mood to hear prayers from his followers. If we pick any random
place and make it a church in the name of the Lord, then what's

the point of building churches? I've seen pictures of beautiful churches in all parts of the world. There must be a purpose in building them, don't you think?

*Liao:* A lot of people refuse to attend services at those beautiful churches because they are controlled by the government's Religious Affairs Bureau.

*Ho:* Does it matter? The holy figure on the cross above the pulpit is my Lord, whether it was above the pulpit at a government church or inside a living room. It's not President Hu Jintao or Chairman Mao.

*Liao:* Well . . .

*Ho:* People in your age group are too political. You guys are too interested in politics. It's different with my generation. Sometimes it bothers me. I attended a house church one time. When we were reading the Bible, a minister or a church elder suddenly stood up. Without getting everyone's approval, he started to deliver a political statement and then asked everyone to pray for so-and-so who had died for the Lord, and then so-and-so who had been arrested by the government. He also asked us to pray for the sins of the government. He totally changed the mood of the gathering, making it depressing and tragic. Several members started to cry after hearing his political plea. I guess I was too young and didn't have that much experience. I felt awkward. I thought, *Why don't we let God do God's work and Caesar do Caesar's? Why do we always mix the two?* The government wants to politicize religion, and some Christians are doing the same thing. These things kill my spiritual appetite.

*Liao:* Well, that's an interesting perspective. Do you know a Christian called Wang Yi? I wonder what his response would be to your argument.

*Ho:* I've heard of Wang Yi. He lives in Chengdu, right? Isn't he the head of the Christian fellowship group called Autumn Blessing? He's a well-known independent intellectual and constitutionalist or something. The Communist Party is keeping a close eye on him, I'm sure. I think his group has been raided by police a couple of times.

*Liao:* Yes. There is another writer, Yu Jie. He's a Christian in Beijing. They are all talented intellectuals and quite brave. They are not afraid of arrest or imprisonment.

*Ho:* There are a lot of talented intellectuals within government churches too. Some people choose to be outspoken, and others choose to be low-key. Some want to fight the political fight, and others want to stay away from politics. That's the reality. I've seen Reverend Yuan Zhiming's documentary film, *The Cross: Jesus in China*. I think it's very biased. He focuses too much on history. Chairman Mao and Deng Xiaoping have been dead a long time. Most Chinese don't care about Communism or revolution anymore. Even the Communist officials don't care much about Communism—like the saying goes, they sell dog meat under the label of a sheep's head. Those Communist officials send their children to the West to receive a different type of education. So why do we still waste our time finding fault with this government? It already feels very insecure for its criminal past. It's better not to provoke the commies.

Maybe I get too much information in my head. Since my brain has limited gigabytes of memory, I just spit them out without filtering. Sorry, I hope it doesn't offend old folks like you. I need to delete some unnecessary files in my head, I guess. Luckily, I have Jesus as my guide. I'm all focused. I think if I keep upgrading my mind, I will do just fine.

*Liao:* Do you use a proxy server to get onto overseas websites?

*Ho:* Of course.

*Liao:* Are you aware of Liu Xiaobo and a document that he and others have drafted? It's called "Charter 08." It's like a declaration to promote democracy and human rights, including the right to religious freedom. Many well-known Chinese intellectuals have signed their names to the document.

*Ho:* You don't need a proxy to access and read "Charter 08." I saw it posted on several domestic websites. The police keep removing it, but more postings pop up. For a while, they couldn't seem to keep up the pace.

*Liao:* Are you in favor of the views outlined in "Charter 08"?

*Ho:* For the long term, I'm in favor of it, but I don't support it in the short term. It won't go very far because it doesn't have grassroots support. But I have to say that it was such damn hooligan behavior to arrest Liu Xiaobo before Christmas and then sentence him to eleven years in jail. Sorry, as a Christian, I shouldn't swear, but I think God will forgive me this time. You know, Liu Xiaobo didn't swear. He expressed his view in a civilized manner. Even if the government doesn't agree with him, they shouldn't lock him up. What are they going to do next? For my generation, Han Han is considered an outspoken writer. He is my hero and a hero for thousands of young people today. He's written some very sharp political commentaries. Are they going to jail him too? After Liu Xiaobo serves out his sentence, he'll be sixty. Even if democracy does arrive in China by then, he'll be too old to do anything. He could join the church, get baptized and ordained, and then become a church minister. In this way, he could preach to others. Otherwise, I don't see any other way out for him, do you?

Look, he belongs to a higher level, the level of professors. I would be in the category of junior student. If you use the computer as a metaphor, he's like a Pentium 6 or Pentium 7 while I'm only a Pentium 2. He is way ahead of me and I'm never going to be his match, but if you listen, he and others like him make sense.

## Acknowledgments

In 2005, Wu Yongsheng, an elder at Fuyintang, the oldest Protestant church in Dali, compiled a book, *The History of Christianity in Dali*, which listed the names of missionaries who had reached the region from around the world, from the mid-1800s to 1949, in order to preach the Gospel. Since many were known only by their Chinese names, it is not surprising that their English names are misspelled, incomplete, or missing. This book is dedicated to the memories of those who lived and preached in Yunnan.

考克宏 Archibald Colquhoun, 1882
斯蒂文 Frederick Arthur Steven, 1882
歐文.史蒂文生 Owen Stevenson, 1882
喬治安德魯 George Andrew, 1882
約翰.史密斯 John Smith, 1885
德史多福卡 F. Theodore Foucar, 1886
哈裏特.史密斯 Harriett Smith, 1890
約翰安德森 John Anderson, 1892
安德森小姐 E. M. D. Anderson, 1892
瑪麗.博克斯 Marie Box, 1895
辛普森小姐 A. M. Simpson, 1895
西比爾.瑞特 Sybil M.E. Reid, 1896

約翰 John Kuhn, 1900
格蘭漢姆 L. Graham, 1900
尼克斯 S. M. E. Nicholls, 1900
郭秀峰 Arthur G. Nicholls, 1900
辛普森 William Wallace Simpson, 1900
桑德斯 A. H. Sanders, 1901
馬錫齡夫婦 No recorded English name, 1901
理查.威廉姆斯 Richard Williams, 1902
哈科特.麥克裏 Hector Mclean, 1902
安選三 William James Embery, 1902
邁克裏 Hector Mclean, 1903
克拉克醫生 Dr. W. T. Clark, 1903
波特小姐 Ethel A. Potter, 1907
王懷仁 George E. Metcalf, 1907
內勒小姐 E. E. Naylor, 1907
海克托 Ms. Hector, 1907
克拉澤小姐 A. Kratzer, 1911
艾德加夫婦 Mr. and Mrs. Edgar, 1912
克萊門 A. J. Clement, 1912
坎寧海姆 J. D. Cunningham, 1912
達真塞勒小姐 Miss Dukesher, 1902
韓純中夫婦 Mr. and Mrs. W. J. Hanna, 1912
富能仁 J. O. Fraser, 1919
楊思惠 Allyn Cooke, 1919
普照恩 No recorded English name, 1919
赫德祿夫婦 Mr. and Mrs. F. S. Hatton, 1926
肯特小姐 D. S. Hatton, 1926
楊志英 John Kuhn, 1930
海富生醫生 Dr. Stuart Harverson, 1933
梁錫生夫婦 Mr. and Mrs. William A. Allen, 1931
馬耀華 Australian, no recorded English name, 1934

柏牧師夫婦 Norwegian, no recorded English name, 1934
何美食 Ted Holmes, 1934
施倫英夫婦 Mr. and Mrs. A. W. Snow, 1940
戴德樂夫婦 Mr. and Mrs. Harold Taylor, 1940
美德純 Jessie McDonald, 1941
鮑文廉 Frances E. Powell, 1941
施愛仁 M. E. Soltau, 1941
馬光啟 Doris M. L. Madden, 1941
趙立德夫婦 Mr. and Mrs. Raymond Joyce, 1946
毛文熙夫婦 No recorded English name, 1948
辛醫生 Dr. Myrtle J. Hinkhouse
塗約翰 Dr. John K. Toop
塗威廉 Dr. William. J. Toop
羅教師 D. W. Burrows
何莉莉 L. Hamer
畢麗蓉 Emma Blott
萬醫生 Dr. Watson
倪護士 Australian, no recorded English name
溫教師 Norwegian, no recorded English name

This book would not have been possible without the assistance of Dr. Sun, who during a two-year period accompanied Liao on trips to the villages in Yunnan and introduced him to the Christian communities there. My thanks also goes to those brave and tenacious Chinese Christians who bared their hearts to Liao Yiwu and whose extraordinary life stories inspired him to write this book.

I am also grateful to Yu Jie, a Christian and a well-known independent literary critic, for his support. Pastor John Zhang, at the San Mateo–based Bay Area Reformed Evangelical Church, has been actively involved in the Christian movement in China. His organization, Humanitarian China, has raised funds for Li Linshan, the "Cancer

Patient" featured in the book, and also arranged for Dr. Sun to stay in the United States after the government banned his missions in Yunnan.

Of course, I am indebted to my wonderful agent, Peter Bernstein, and his wife, Amy, for their confidence and persistence. I am grateful that Tim Cribb in Hong Kong featured several of Liao's writings in the *Asia Literary Review* and enhanced the book through his thorough editing. I also appreciate the editorial assistance and input from my friends Colin McMahon and Monica Eng at the *Chicago Tribune* and Robert Crowley in Springfield, Illinois.

This book also benefited from the consultations I had with Reverend Michael Bradley of the Chicago Archdiocese. Reverend Bradley meticulously reviewed the whole manuscript and patiently answered my queries, some of which required extensive research on his part.

Additionally, I am also grateful to Martin-Liao Tienchi, president of the Independent Chinese PEN Centre, for advocating and supporting independent Chinese writers such as Liao Yiwu.

In the early 1990s, Bruce Kinette and his mother, Vera, took me to several church services in order to help me understand American culture. Bruce also gave me a NIV Study Bible, which I used during the translation of this book. All the English equivalents for the biblical references cited in the original Chinese are based on the NIV version.

Over the years, my friend Gerhard Dierkes in Berlin has quietly helped me with my translation work and supplied many of Liao's pictures.

In the same month the book was finished, my friend Kate Durham gave birth to a beautiful girl, Angie, who has brought tremendous joy to Kate and Craig, and has brightened the lives of friends like me. I hope that Angie will grow up in a peaceful world, where people continue to respect each other's faiths and are allowed to practice their religions freely.

Linda Yu, who generously shared the story of her late grandmother, a devout Christian, helped me understand the Christian movement in the pre-Communist era. I am also grateful to Tao Zhang, Caren and Dale Thomas, and David Alexander for their warm support.

Most of all, I want to thank our editor Mickey Maudlin, whose interest in the topic and foresight made this book possible. Kathyrn Renz and Lisa Zuniga efficiently moved the editorial process forward, and for this, I am grateful.

Finally, I wish to thank my friends and co-workers Thaddeus Woosley, Hans Van Heukelum, Andrew Delaney, Kelly Drinkwine, and Tory Neff for their support and friendship.